Netscape™ for Macintosh®

Springer

New York
Berlin
Heidelberg
Barcelona
Budapest
Hong Kong
London
Milan
Paris
Santa Clara
Singapore
Tokyo

Richard Raucci

Netscape™ for Macintosh®

A hands-on configuration and set-up guide for popular Web browsers

With 183 Illustrations

 Springer

Richard Raucci
435 Eureka Street
San Francisco, CA 94114 USA
rraucci@well.com
rraucci@interramp.com
http://www.well.com/Community/rraucci/raucci.html

Library of Congress Cataloging-in-Publication Data
Raucci, Richard.
        Netscape for Macintosh : a hands-on configuration and set-up guide
    for popular Web browsers / Richard Raucci.
        p. cm.
    Includes bibliographical references and index.
    1. Netscape. 2. World Wide Web (Information
retrieval system) 3. Internet (Computer network) I. Title.
TK5105.882.R38 1996
025.04–dc20   95-47549

Printed on acid-free paper.

Production managed by Bill Imbornoni; manufacturing supervised by Jacqui Ashri.

9 8 7 6 5 4 3 2 1
ISBN-13: 978-0-387-94662-7   e-ISBN-13: 978-1-4612-2382-5
DOI: 10.1007/ 978-1-4612-2382-5

Contents

Introduction

Netscape, since its introduction as successor to the original Web browser Mosaic, has captured the lion's share of the Web browser market. Its advanced features make it the premier Internet navigation tool you can use. The Internet, in turn, is the real Info Superhighway—a place to exchange information of all types with people all over the world, find files, search extensive databases, play games, and more.

The Macintosh is ideally suited to take advantage of the features of a Web browser like Netscape and the rich informational resources available over the Net. Most Macs are already set to run with the basic capabilities you'll need, including graphics and sound. All it takes is an inexpensive modem, an Internet access provider, and a copy of Netscape. This book will show you how to set up and configure Netscape, as well as a representative variety of other Web browsers for Macintosh, including NCSA MacMosaic, PLUSMosaic from White Pine Software (a version of Enhanced NCSA MacMosaic from Spyglass), MacWeb from TradeWave, and InterCon's NetShark.

Netscape followed the successful introduction of the original Web browser, NCSA Mosaic. This was developed at the National Center for Supercomputing Applications at the University of Illinois, Champaign-Urbana as a part of the World Wide Web

(WWW) project. The WWW was conceived as a way to manage the vast amounts of information on the Internet. Mosaic was designed to be a Web browser, an application that could load information from a variety of sources (server file directories, text, and images, for example) into a common interface. Previously, Internet information of different types had to be accessed from several different applications, resulting in too many steps for the process to be efficient (for example, you had to download a picture file from a remote site, then open it up in a paint program to view it; this meant that you couldn't *see* the image before you downloaded it).

Web browsers changed all of this. Finally, indexed multimedia information could be displayed in a common interface. Browsers not only display picture and text files internally, they also incorporate a hypertext interface. This means that a Netscape home page (an Internet document) can contain links to other Internet sites and information. This interface is in a standard point-and-click format. Highlighted images and text contain the links. To continue the example given above, Netscape can now load in a series of small, thumbnail in-line images for browsing pictures at a remote site, so you can see what the picture looks like before downloading. Each small picture can be linked to a larger version; clicking on the picture will start the download automatically, and Netscape will even launch an external viewer (when configured properly) to display the big picture.

Great stuff! Also great was at the time that the original Web browsers were designed, the programmers at NCSA decided that the technology had to be available for all users. Versions for the three main platforms (Windows, Macintosh, and Unix) were developed at the same time by different teams. The Macintosh version grew out of this, and Netscape's first releases included a strong Mac version. Further development included a PowerPC Native port, and development work on including plug-in support for standard Mac software technologies (like QuickTime).

Netscape Communications' strong focus on compelling graphics in their Web sites—used as an adjunct to the software releases —is a sure sign that they won't leave the Mac behind. The Mac is still the best design tool available, and it runs Netscape to its full potential as a client as well. Netscape's partnership with cable companies developing home video versions of Internet access via cable modems also would seem to bode well for the Macintosh. There's no better operating system than MacOS to keep the future Netscape platforms easy to use and comfortable to navigate with for all levels of users.

1
Getting Started

To get started using a Web browser like Netscape on the Macintosh, you'll first need to make sure your system meets the minimum configuration. Most alternate browsers will use the same Mac setup as Netscape for Macintosh. These all are being developed as either 68K or PowerPC Native applications, or combined versions that will run on both systems.

68K or PowerPC?

The 68K code base is what's standard for pre-PowerPC Macintoshes that use the Motorola series of 68XXX processors. Native PowerPC software is designed to run on the RISC PowerPC CPU at much faster speeds, with support for advanced operating system features like multitasking. The benefits of running a Web browser in PowerPC Native mode are clear, but that doesn't mean you absolutely need a PowerPC system to run Netscape well. The Mac's design makes 68K standard software run well. You should also realize that PowerPC Mac systems incorporate a 68K code emulator, meaning they can run both types of software.

System 6 and 7

Most browsers need the more advanced features of System 7, and some also need the features in System 7.5 (not System 7.1). This may be even more true for certain helper applications that Netscape uses to view pictures and play sound files. You could conceivably use Web browsers with System 6, but you may not be able to get the same amount of functionality. System 7 will use more of your Mac's main memory, so you may want to consider increasing your system RAM or using virtual memory (use the RamDoubler utility to increase this even further).

How Much Mac Do I Need?

The Macintosh setup you'll need to run Netscape and other Web browsers is fairly straightforward. Most Macs capable of running in 256 color mode are perfectly suitable, from the Mac II (with an 8-bit color card installed) to the latest Performa. Macs that can support "thousands of colors" mode (and beyond) are more suitable for Web sites with intensive graphics. A screen resolution of 640 × 480 (the base level for most Macintoshes) is fairly good for viewing Netscape, but you should see if your system is capable of 800 × 600. DTP systems with 21-inch monitors running at 1120 × 1280 are also a plus. The more resolution you can afford, the more of a Web page you can see on the screen at one time without scrolling.

Use the Options button in the Monitors Control Panel to change your system's resolution settings. You may need to switch to a monitor that supports higher screen settings, add a higher-resolution video card, or increase your system's video RAM (for Macs with built-in video).

Systems that can run grayscale video (like Powerbooks) are also suitable for limited Netscape use. You can also use a 640 × 400 screen (as on the Color Classic and some Powerbooks), but you may find yourself a bit cramped.

Make sure you have at least 2 MB of RAM above what you'll need for your operating system to allow Netscape enough memory to run properly. For example, an older Mac running System 7.5 could need at least 4–6 MB of total system RAM to run the

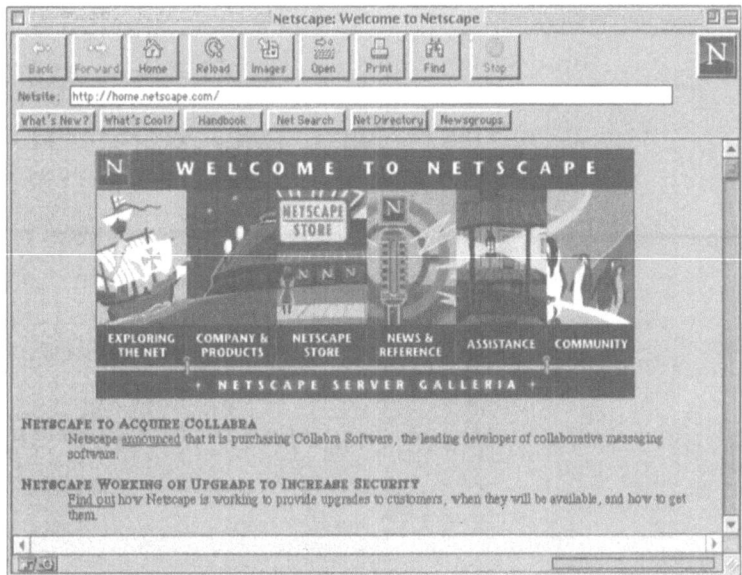

FIGURE 1.1.
640 × 480
Netscape.

FIGURE 1.2.
The Options panel
under the Monitors
Control Panel.

OS and Netscape as well (and you'd be better off with 8 MB of RAM). A newer PowerPC Mac with a large number of System Extensions and Control Panels installed may need 12–16 MB of total system RAM.

To check your system, go to the Apple Menu and launch the About This Macintosh box. It will tell you how much RAM you have installed, and also show how much memory your system software is taking up. You can subtract the latter from the former to see how much RAM you have for Web browser applications, and whether you need to remove some unused System Extensions and Control Panels (to reduce the amount of memory your system software is taking up), or add more RAM.

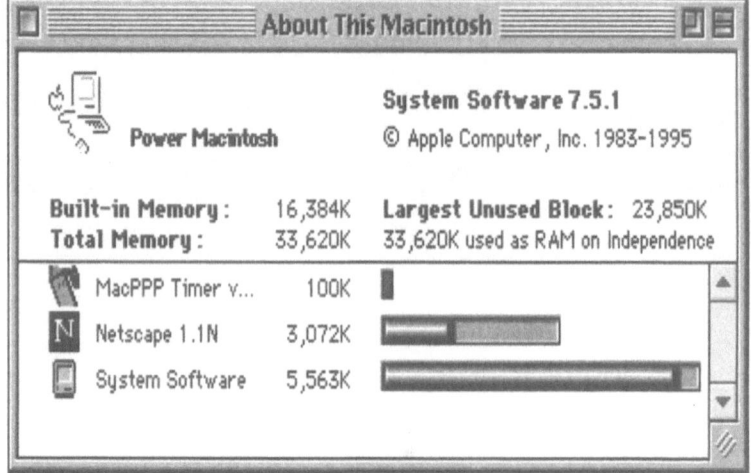

FIGURE 1.3.
The About This Macintosh dialog box.

You can also use the Memory Control Panel to access virtual memory to increase RAM. This allows you to use a portion of your hard drive space as RAM. It's somewhat slower than actual RAM, but it certainly costs less. If you're low on RAM and have a large hard drive, you might want to give this a try. This only works on Macs with a 68030 CPU or greater.

You can remove unused System Extensions and Control Panels to free up system RAM just by dragging them out of the relevant folders in the System Folder. Make new folders called "Disabled Extensions" and "Disabled Control Panels," and park them there. Make absolutely sure you know what you're doing; you may render some of your hardware and applications unusable if you remove the wrong things. Reboot to see how much RAM you've conserved.

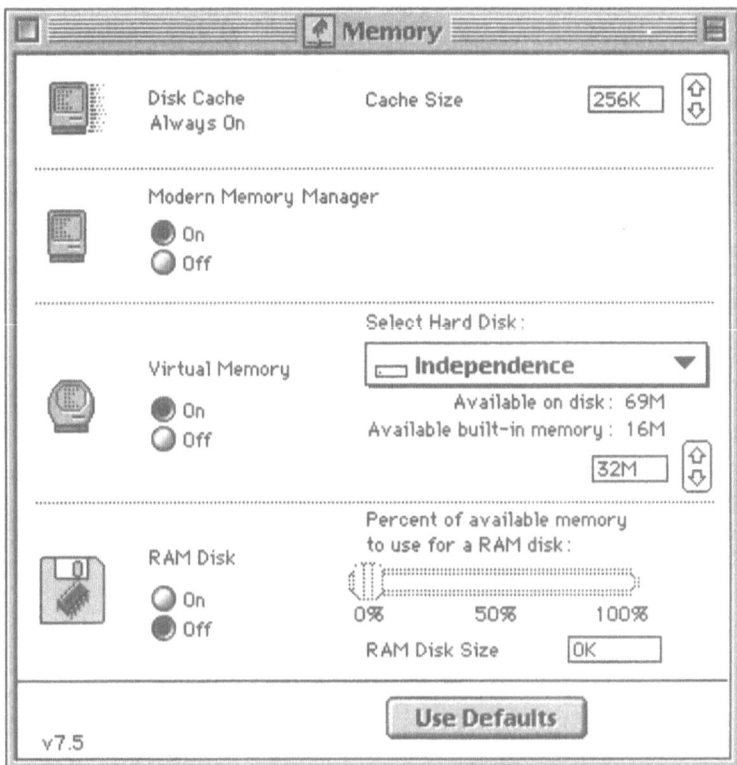

FIGURE 1.4.
The Memory Control
Panel.

In System 7.5, you can use the Extensions Manager Control Panel to disable Extensions and Control Panels without having to move them. Remove the check from the names of the ones you want to turn off, and reboot. You can also save different configurations with this Control Panel, or turn everything on and off. Multiple configurations can allow you to keep a set for running Netscape only, turning off extensions you know you won't be using while running it, and allowing you to restore your normal work setup later. (See Figure 1.5.)

You'll need about 2 MB of hard disk space for a Web browser like Netscape, and about 10 MB of space for associated helper applications. Applications can come in three types: 68K, PowerPC Native, and FAT. A FAT application will run on either a PowerPC or a 68K Mac, and may be the only version of some software. You can conserve space by keeping those versions that will run on your system only.

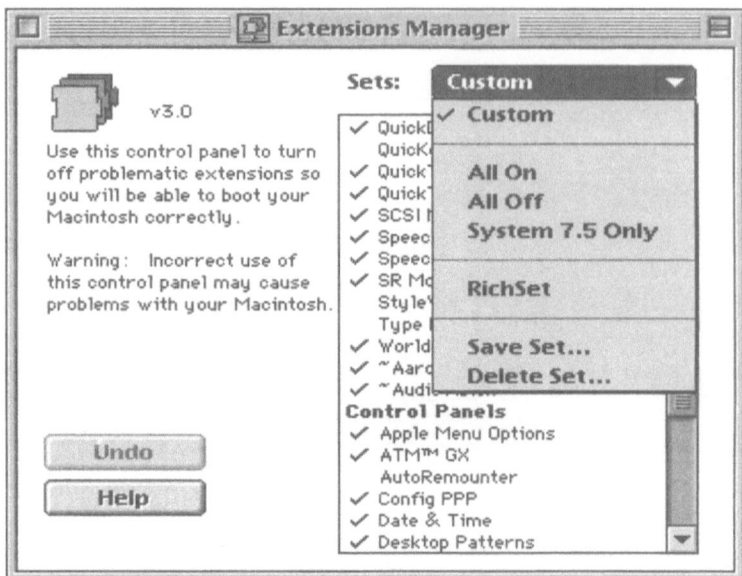

FIGURE 1.5.
Extensions Manager
Control Panel.

Where to Get It

Netscape for Macintosh is available from Netscape Communications' Web site in a trial version, and also in a retail version from selected software stores and catalogs. The retail version of Netscape includes selected Internet Access Provider trial accounts. You can use FTP to download a copy at ftp://ftp. netscape.com if you already have an Internet connection. Note that some Web browsers need the header ftp:// in the address line to reach an FTP server directly, but FTP programs like Fetch do not. Just use ftp.netscape.com instead. A small hint: try ftp2. netscape.com and ftp3.netscape.com if the main servers are busy, and also look for alternate sites to FTP Netscape that are closer to your location.

You can also use Netscape's home page to download Netscape from the server closest to you, if you already have a Web browser and access account. Just go to home.netscape.com and follow the Netscape Now links.

Other Web browsers available over the Net include NCSA Mac-Mosaic, available from ftp://ftp.ncsa.uiuc.edu in the /Mosaic /Mac directory, and TradeWave's MacWeb, at ftp://ftp.einet. net in the /einet/mac directory. You can download a trial version of Intercon's NetShark from their FTP site (which includes a full

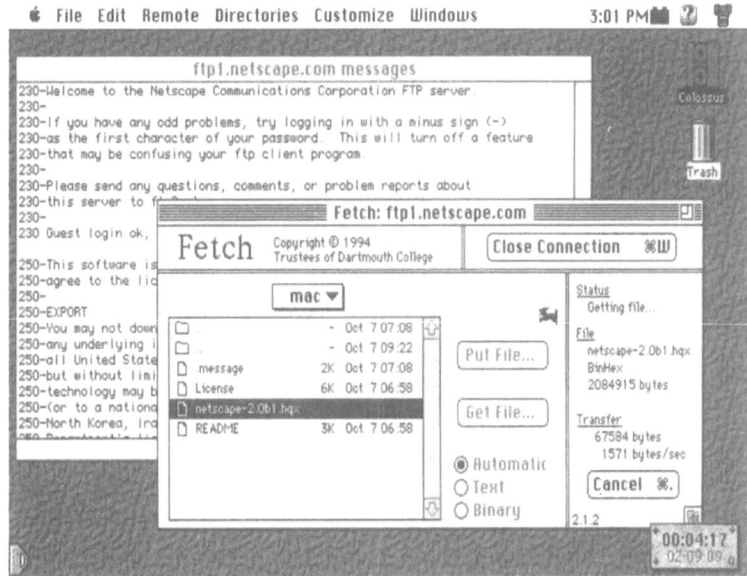

FIGURE 1.6.
Using the Fetch FTP program to access Netscape's FTP site.

set of Internet tools, including MacTCP) at `ftp://inter.shark.net`.

You can also find versions of NCSA Mosaic for the Macintosh from Spyglass Corporation (typically known as "Enhanced Spyglass Mosaic") bundled as a part of commercial Internet software packages. These include White Pine's PLUSMosaic (`www.wpine.com`) and Software Ventures' Internet Valet (`www.svcdudes.com`).

Regardless of which browser you start with, a good Internet Access Provider connection should allow you to use any browser you want, including Netscape. This is the main difference between an on-line service (like AmericaOnline) and a true Internet Access Provider (like PSI).

Helper Applications

Helper applications are those programs that allow Netscape to view images, play sound files, and run animations and movies. These can be configured quite easily from Netscape's Options/ Preferences panel. Use the drop-down list to move to the Helper Applications section, and you can see a wide range of file formats that the Web browser already knows about. (See Figure 1.7.)

The Helper Applications already preconfigured for use with

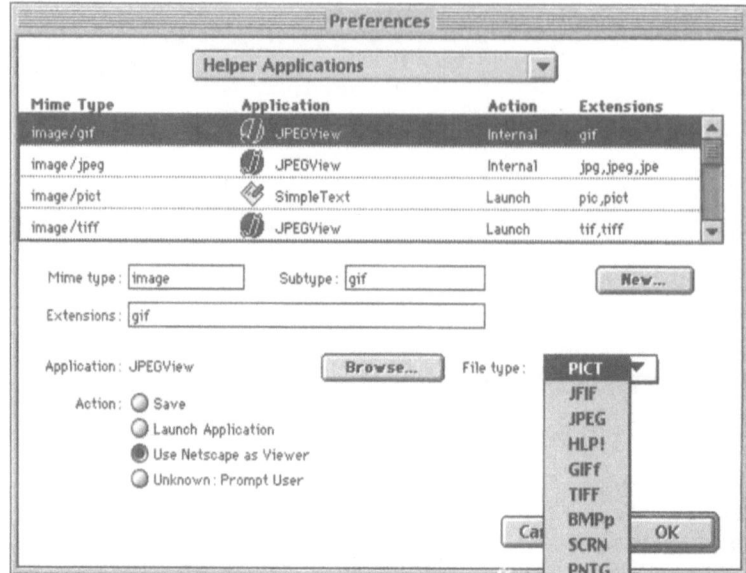

FIGURE 1.7.
Netscape's Options/Preferences panel for Helper Applications.

Netscape are listed here. Use this as a guide to know which ones you should download and install. Netscape's home page has links to the most common Helper Application Web and FTP sites; use it to configure the following applications. Click on the Helper Applications link under the Assistance section at the Netscape home page for more information.

Although Netscape already knows how to load certain image file formats natively, like JPEG and GIF files, other images at a Web site may be in different formats, like the Mac standard TIFF format. You can use an image display program like JPEGView to view these files externally. You can also use JPEGView to view files off-line that Netscape can handle internally, so you can continue to browse the Web site. Just download the file instead, and drag it on the JPEGView icon. JPEGView will also allow you to see formats like Windows' BMP and Mac PICT files.

The Sparkle program allows you to view MPEG and QuickTime animations and movies. You'll need to set Netscape to use Sparkle for QuickTime; it's already used as a default for MPEG. The latest versions only run under System 7.5.

QuickTime is Apple's multimedia movie and animation protocol. Find out more about it at Apple's official QuickTime Web site, http://quicktime.apple.com. It's included with System 7.5, and you can download and watch QuickTime movies from Web

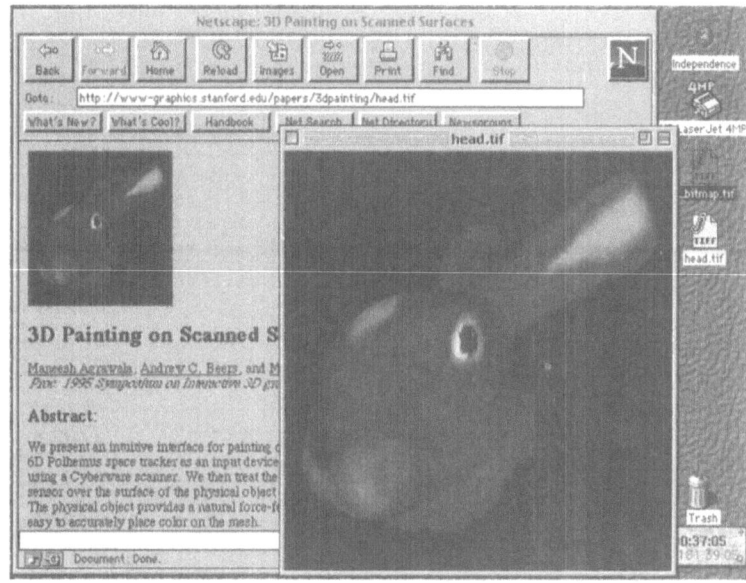

FIGURE 1.8.
JPEGView launching
an external viewer.

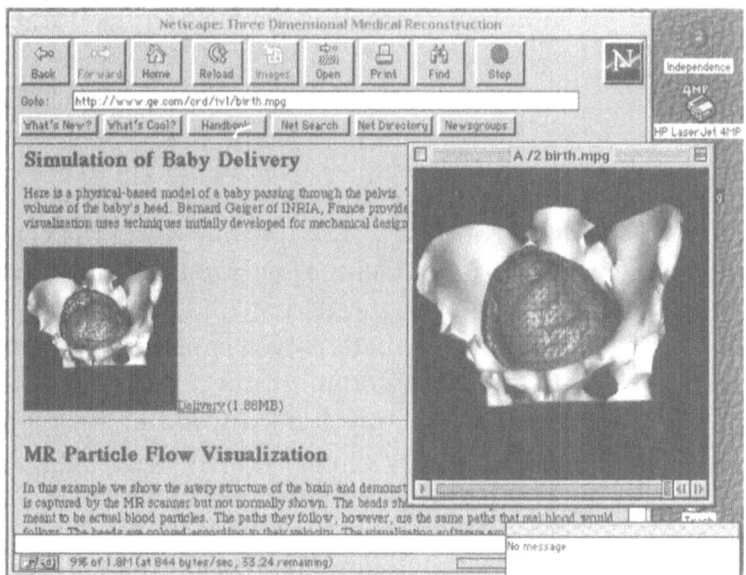

FIGURE 1.9.
Sparkle running an
MPEG animation.

sites using SimpleText or a program called SimplePlayer (avail-able from Apple's Web sites). You may want to use an alternate movie player (including Sparkle or Apple's MoviePlayer); you'll have to reconfigure Netscape to use the new player.

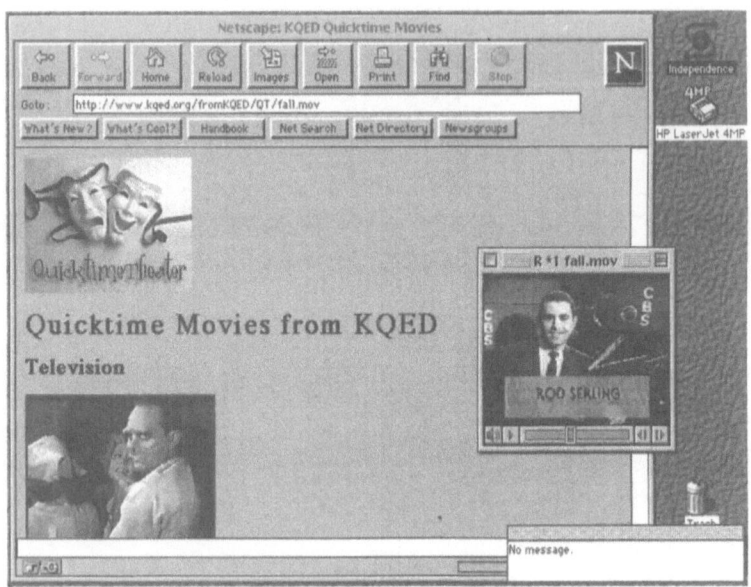

FIGURE 1.10.
Netscape launching a QuickTime movie (using Sparkle) from a Web site.

Apple also recently developed QuickTimeVR, a panoramic view QuickTime format for scenes that you can rotate through in three dimensions, and zoom in and out on. You'll need to load the QuickTimeVR player from Apple's Web site and set it as your QuickTime player in Netscape to make use of it (it will also play standard QuickTime movies). You can also download the QTVR movies and view them off-line using the QTVR Player.

Use SoundMachine as a good, all-round audio player. Netscape is already configured for it, and the program can handle standard Mac sound formats, as well as some of the more common formats for sound files found on the Internet (the .AU and .AIFF types especially). All you'll need to do is download the program and install it, and it will work with Netscape.

The RealAudio file format/application system allows you to play audio files as they are downloading, instead of having to wait through a long file transfer first. It's a significant develop-ment. The player application automatically installs to Netscape's Preferences section as a Helper Application, and is very easy to

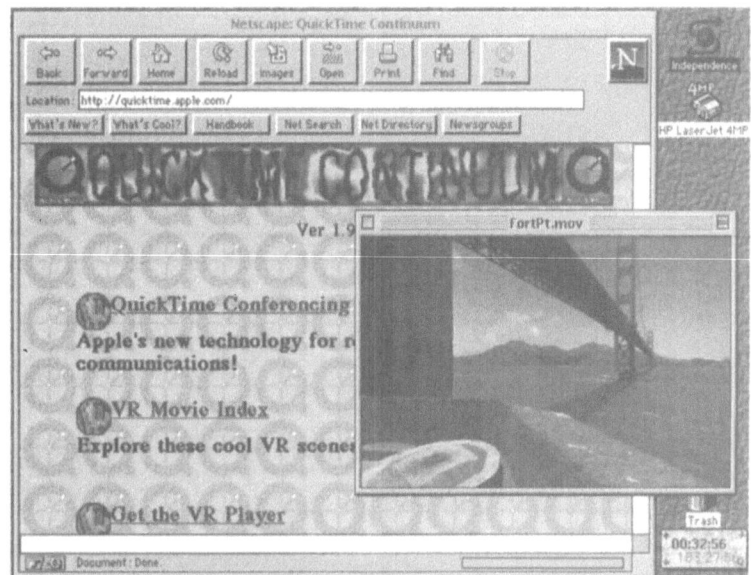

FIGURE 1.11.
Netscape launching
QuickTimeVR movie.

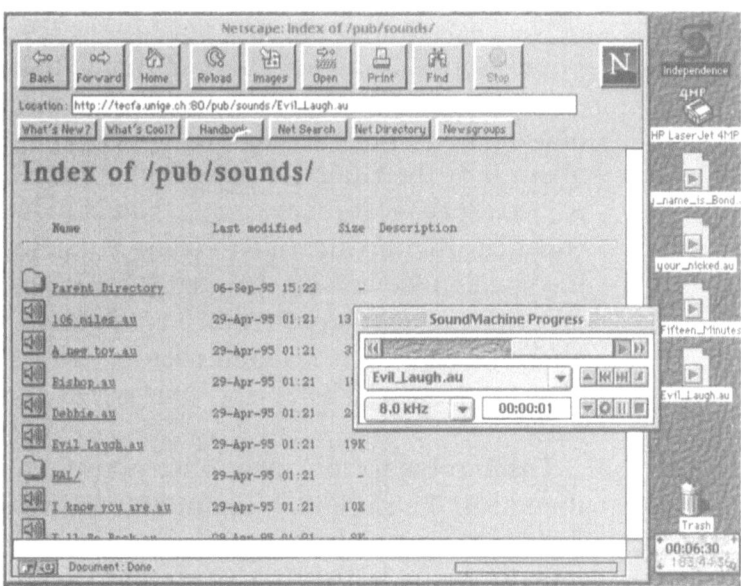

FIGURE 1.12.
SoundMachine in
action.

set up. You can find it at the RealAudio home page, `http://www.realaudio.com`.

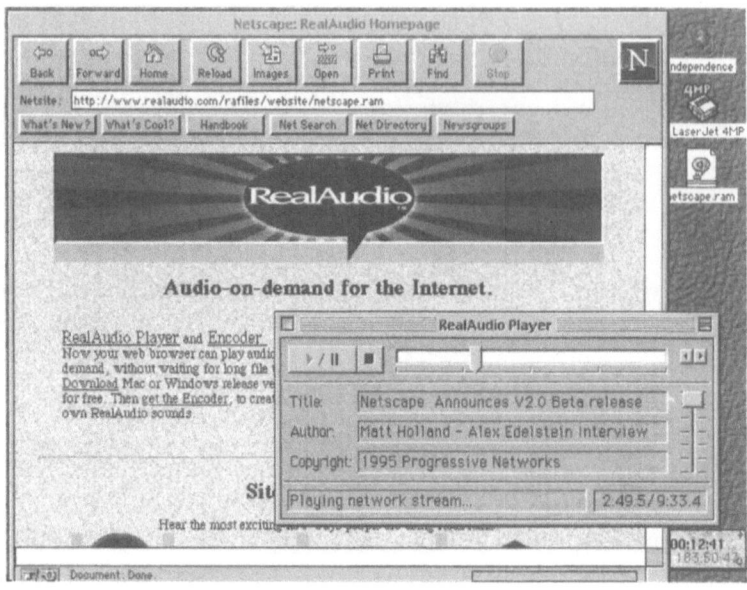

FIGURE 1.13.
RealAudio in action.

Some files on the Internet will be in the PostScript format. There are a number of ways that Netscape can handle these; one of the easiest is to use an application like Adobe Illustrator or Photoshop as a viewer. This can put a strain on your system resources, however. There are also shareware PostScript viewers in development, most notably Ghostscript. You can find out more about it at the Ghostscript Web site, `http://www.glyphic.com/glyphic/projects/macgs.html`. You can also use the Adobe Acrobat Distiller application to convert the PostScript file to a PDF file you can view using Acrobat Reader or Exchange. Note that all of these techniques require configuring Netscape to use the alternate viewers (the default setup, using TeachText, is unsuitable for viewing PostScript, unless you like to look at a lot of code).

The Acrobat format mentioned above is a good way to get documents in their original format over the World Wide Web. Apple has done a great job of providing product information sheets that look the same as their paper counterparts, for example. Best of all, you can download the Acrobat Reader program at no cost from Adobe (and selected sites, like Apple's).

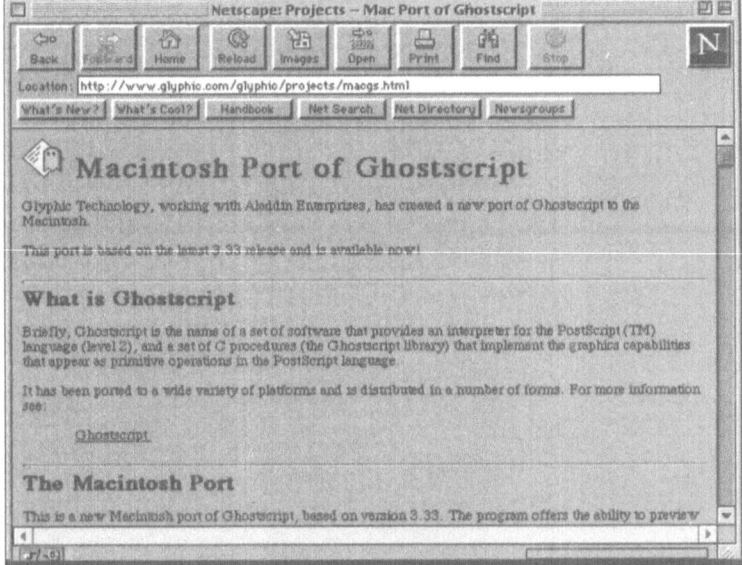

FIGURE 1.14.
The Ghostscript Web
site.

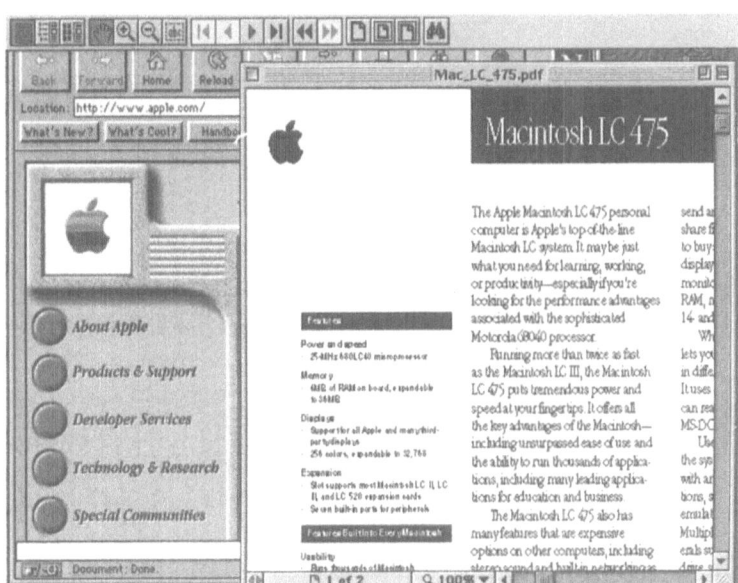

FIGURE 1.15.
Acrobat Reader
viewing an Apple
product info sheet.

You can place most of your Helper Applications in the same folder. After you install Netscape for the first time, create a folder called "Helper Applications," and install the programs to this folder each time you add one. It'll help keep your desktop uncluttered, and you'll know where to look for them later (if you want to view downloaded files off-line).

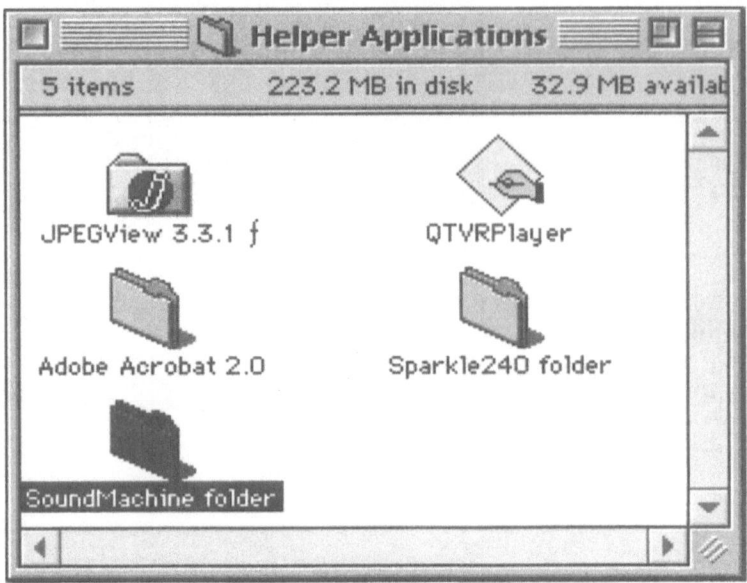

FIGURE 1.16.
Helper Applications folder view.

To download helper applications under Netscape, hold down the option key while clicking on a file transfer link. Netscape will then save the file to your hard drive. The files will mostly be in a BinHex format. This format is used to maintain Mac file integrity when downloading program files over the Net. Use a shareware program called BinHex to convert the files to their binary equivalents (usually Stuffit or CompactPro archives). You can then decompress the files and run their installation programs. CompactPro can also decode BinHexed files by itself. Also note that some file archives can be in self-extracting format, meaning that you won't need a decompression utility to use (but it's best to keep Stuffit and CompactPro on hand anyway).

In certain cases, files for the Mac available over the Net will be in a disk image format. This allows a company to set up software releases that will ultimately look the same as if you'd received them on disk. Apple is most notable for providing software updates in this format. You'll need a utility called DiskCopy to move the disk images to floppies. This means you may have a long trail to follow when downloading software over the Internet, possibly from BinHex to Stuffit to Disk Image to Floppy, but it all works well and preserves file integrity.

There are good sites for obtaining these programs at the University of Texas (`http://wwwhost.ots.utexas.edu/mac/`) and the Info-Mac archives (`ftp://mirror.apple.com/mirrors/Info-Mac.Archive/`), in the Compression, Translation, Graphics, and Sound Tools directories.

The file formats you'll most encounter over the Web are listed in the following sections.

Image File Formats

.GIF   Graphics Interchange Format, a stand PC picture file format that Netscape for Macintosh can view directly inside its main window.

.JPG   Joint Picture Experts Group compressed image file format that Netscape can view directly, and can also be viewed using JPEGView externally.

.PICT   Standard Mac picture file format, viewable externally in SimpleText (under System 7.5) and JPEGView, and directly in some Web browsers.

Note: There are a lot of image file formats in use on the Internet that will pertain to certain Mac applications beyond those listed above. You may encounter TIFF images, for example, at some sites. Using a program like JPEGView as a default viewer beyond Netscape's internal capabilities is a good idea (it supports PICT, TIFF, and PC .BMP file formats), and Photoshop as a further image-handling program for Netscape might also be worth considering.

Motion Video File Formats

.QT, .MOV   QuickTime file formats. Nearly every Mac is already configured to use QuickTime properly (it's included with System 7.5). QuickTimeVR files need a QuickTime VR player to run them.

.MPG   MPEG (Motion Picture Experts Group) video format. Use Sparkle to view MPEG videos and animations properly.

.AVI   Video for Windows file format. You can use an AVI to QuickTime conversion program (a basic version is included with Sparkle) to convert these files to QuickTime.

Compression Formats

.SIT, .SEA   Alladin Corporation's common compression format for the Mac. Use the Stuffit Deluxe, Extractor, and Stuffit Lite programs to unpack these files. Stuffit can also decode BinHexed files.

.CPT   CompactPro compression format. You can also use CompactPro to decode BinHexed files.

.ZIP   The standard compression format for PCs. Use MacZip or ZipIt to decompress these files.

.tar   UNIX compressed file format (UNIX tar command). Use a Mac Tar program to decompress these files.

.gz   GNUtar, alternate compressed tar file format (gzip command). Use the MacGZIP program for these types of files.

Note: Most .ZIP files pertain only to PC binary files that won't run directly on a Macintosh. You'll probably want to download and decompress only .ZIP files containing documents and picture files in standard formats that Mac programs can handle.

Encodation File Formats

.HQX   The BinHex file format, used to convert Mac binary files into ASCII text.

.UUE   UUencodation, used also to convert binary files to ASCII text (mostly PC or Unix files, however).

Note: As with .ZIP files, files converted to UUencoded format may not be suitable to run on Mac systems after you decode them. Make sure the decoded file will be in a standard Mac file format, or that it's a document or picture file your Mac applications can handle.

Document File Formats

.TXT   Standard ASCII text files (usually README files are in this format).

.DOC   Microsoft Word document format.

.WPD   WordPerfect document format.

.RTF   Rich Text document format, typically with more formatting than ASCII text files.

.PS   PostScript file format.

.PDF   Adobe Acrobat document format.

Note: As with graphics file formats, there are a lot more document file formats than those mentioned here for more specific word processing programs. It's possible to use a program like Microsoft Word or WordPerfect to translate a larger number of Mac document formats. Adobe Acrobat .PDF files need the Acrobat Reader program to view them properly (though native .PDF support is expected in a later version of Netscape). PostScript files on the Internet can be documents, image files, or a combination of both.

2
Netscape and Other Macintosh Web Browsers: A Summary

Netscape provides a standard interface for information available over the Internet. It runs almost like a word processor, but with much more advanced graphics and multimedia capability.

Netscape was developed by Marc Andreeson at Netscape Communications as a follow-up to the original NCSA Mosaic Web browser. You can find it at the Netscape Communications Web site, `http://home.netscape.com`.

Netscape 1.1

The main window for Netscape version 1.1 shows Web documents from across the Internet, including in-line images and text. The large N with the moving graphics at the left top of the window is a progress indicator. It lets you know that a Web document transfer is taking place. You can click on the icon to stop the transfer (or use the Stop button). The Toolbar contains the functions you need to navigate the World Wide Web, including back and forward keys to move between documents, a home button that will always take you back to your default home page, and a button you can use to reload a Web page. There are also buttons for loading images (you can turn off automatic image loading if you have a slow connection), printing documents, and finding text in a Web page.

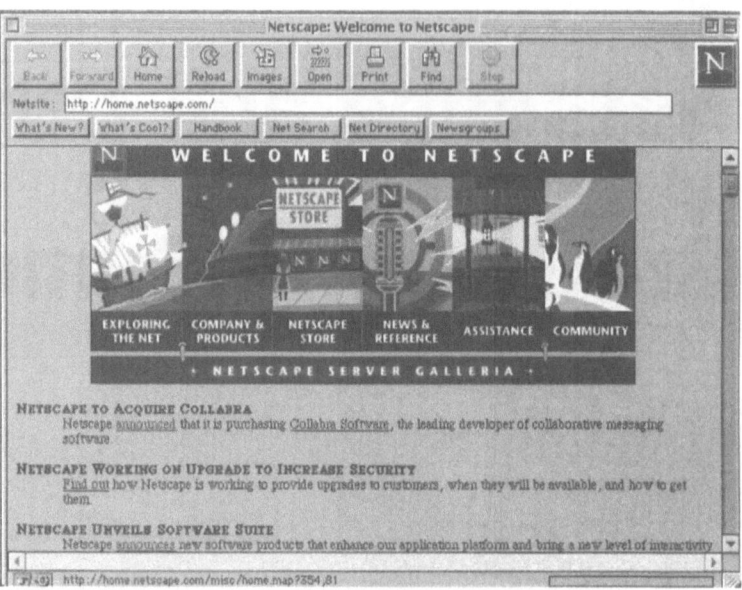

FIGURE 2.1.
Netscape 1.1's main window view.

Below the Toolbar is the location window. This shows the actual address of the Web document that you're currently viewing. You can also use this window to type in a Web address to load, or cut and paste Web addresses from on-line documents. Netscape is also smart enough to figure out most standard header formats, meaning that you don't have to type out all of the address (for example, you can type `www.apple.com` instead of `http://www.apple.com` in this window and Netscape will take it from there).

Netscape also features helpful directory buttons below the location window. These are linked to Netscape Communications Web pages, with sections on What's New and What's Cool, an online Netscape handbook, a page linked to comprehensive Internet search tools,search tools a Net directory, and a link to Usenet newsgroups. You can use the directory buttons to get a good feel for what's available on the World Wide Web.

There's also a progress indicator at the lower left of the main window, a long rectangular box that will fill up as your document transfers into Netscape. At the right bottom of the window (in Netscape 1.1 and above) you'll see a small key; it'll be broken for documents not using Netscape's security features, and complete

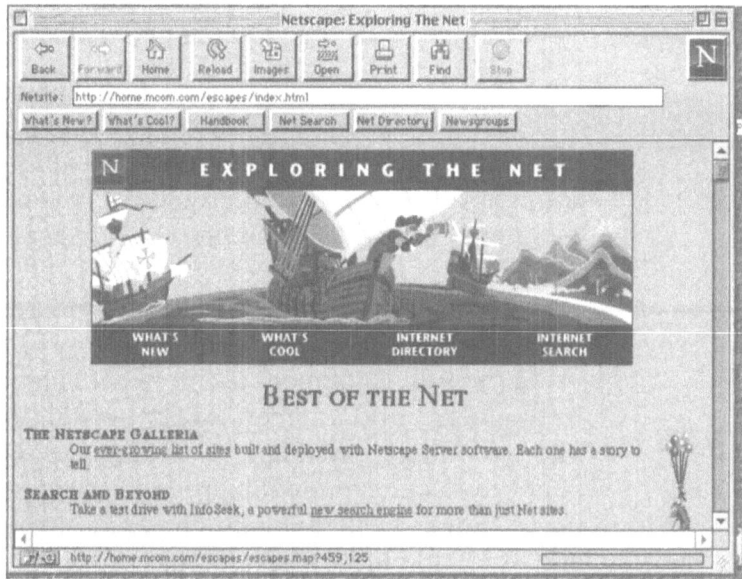

FIGURE 2.2.
Netscape's Best of
the Net page, linked
to the Netscape
directory button
subjects.

for those that do. Between these features you can read short status messages and addresses for hypermedia links in documents (place the mouse pointer over a link and view the address below).

The Netscape File Menu has items for loading URLs (Uniform Request Locators, AKA Web document addresses) and local files (for viewing HTML hypertext documents you may have on your hard drive, or for using Netscape as an image viewer). You can also save a document locally from here (as text or source), send a message including a document address (also optionally including the text of the Web page) by using a small Email panel, and view a Web document's security information. Use the New Window feature to start another main Web browser view. You can connect to multiple Internet sites this way.

The Edit Menu has standard Cut, Copy, and Paste features. You can usually highlight and perform these functions on the text in a Web document (for example, to copy a Web address and paste it into another application). This menu also has a Find function you can use to search Web documents locally.

The View Menu has equivalents for the Reload and Load Images Toolbar items, as well as a View/Source item that will launch a text viewer to show you the HTML code in a Web document. You can set any word processor for use with this menu function, or use the default TeachText/SimpleText program configured for Netscape.

The Go Menu has functions for moving back and forth between Web documents, loading the default home page, and stopping a transfer. There's also a list of most recently viewed pages you can scroll through to go to directly, and a History panel that includes the same type of information, but also features the site address as well.

Bookmarks are a good way to keep interesting Web sites close to hand. You can save a bookmark to any page at any time by using the Add Bookmark menu item. The bookmarks are added to the menu, and you can scroll through them to find a particular site. There's also a View Bookmarks item that opens up a panel you can use to configure your bookmark settings, including setting up nested menus, changing site names and addresses, and exporting/importing alternate bookmark files. You can also use this panel to search through your bookmarks for a particular topic name.

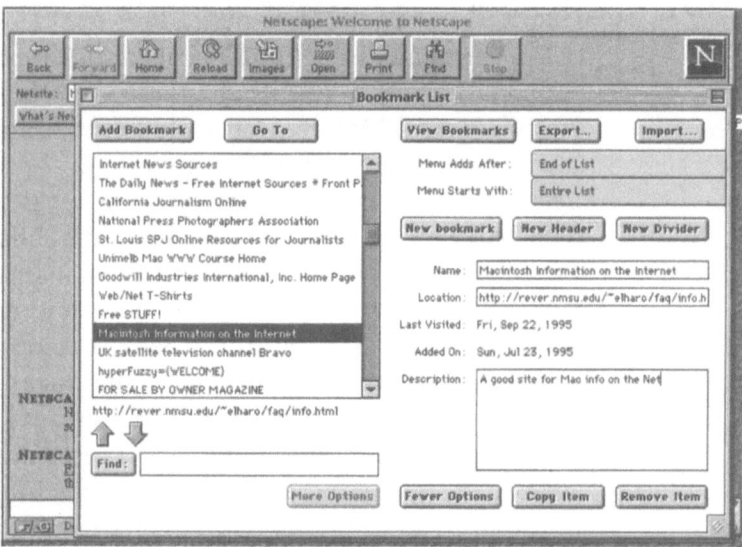

FIGURE 2.3.
Netscape's View Bookmarks panel.

The Options Menu has items that allow you to turn off the Toolbar, the location window, and the directory buttons. This will give you a bit more space in the main viewer window, so that you can view large image files properly. You can still navigate between pages by using the Go Menu. There's also a Preferences item that will load the Preference panel you'll use to configure Netscape. You can scroll through the different sections to set up window and link styles (this is where you can set an alternate home page), font and color usage (here's where you can turn off backgrounds if they clash with the page's text—use a custom gray background instead), and mail and news applications (set up this section with information from your Internet Access Provider in order to use the Mail Document and Usenet Newsgroups functions properly). There are also sections for cache and network settings (useful if Netscape is using too much of your disk space; you can clear out the disk cache at any time from here as well), images and security (for turning automatic image loading on and off and configuring security alert messages), and applications and directories (use this section to set up telnet applications to run automatically from Netscape, and also to configure which word processor to use to view the HTML source in a document). The Helper Applications section is where you'll configure the viewers mentioned in the first chapter. You can also add new data types for use with alternate helper applications here, and extend your Web browser's range.

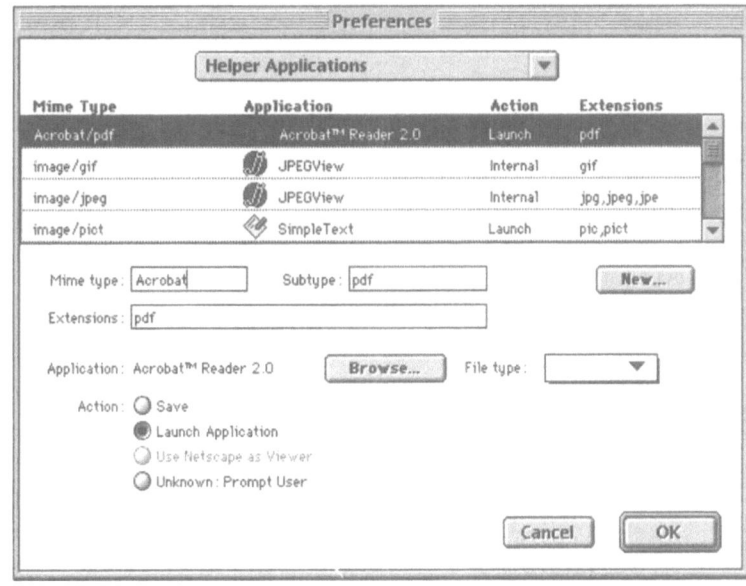

FIGURE 2.4. Netscape's Options/Preferences Helper Applications panel.

The Directory Menu has most of the same items available from the directory buttons, and also includes links to the Netscape Galleria, the Internet White Pages (where you can look up info on users across the Internet), and a section called About the Internet.

The Help Menu has links to Netscape version information, on-line help pages, registration information, release notes, Frequently Asked Questions, and explanations of Netscape's software security protocols.

Netscape also features a floating menu for commonly accessed functions. Just hold down the mouse button for a brief period in the main window to use it (hold it over a link for different functions). Sections include back and forward commands, bookmark utilities, and image viewing, copying, and saving functions.

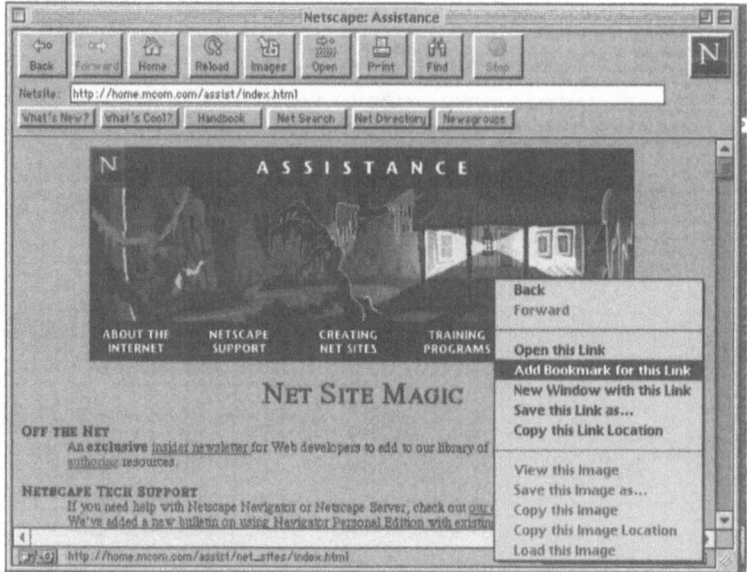

FIGURE 2.5.
Netscape's floating menu over a link.

Netscape 2.0

Netscape 2.0 for Macintosh adds many interesting features. The basic look is the same, but you'll find an improved mail system (Netscape can now store and read your Internet PPP mail directly) and a better News reader.

The bookmark system has also been totally revised with the addition of a floating palette that's much easier to use, and new

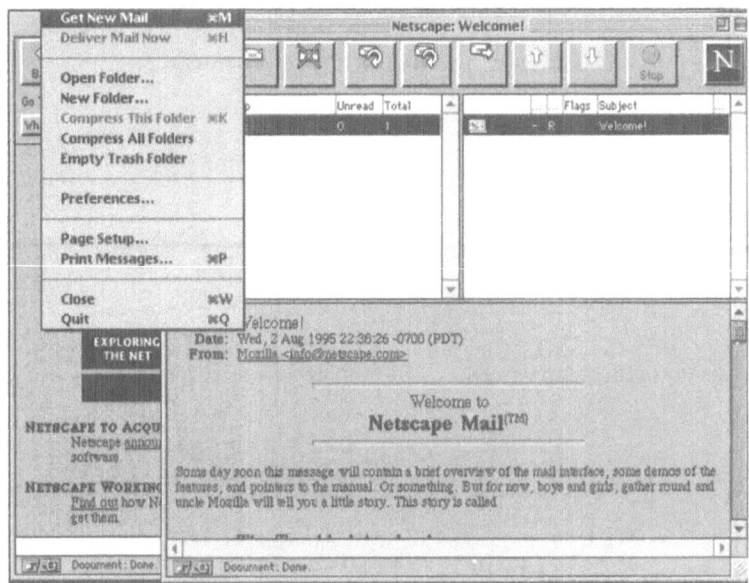

FIGURE 2.6.
Netscape 2.0's mail
system.

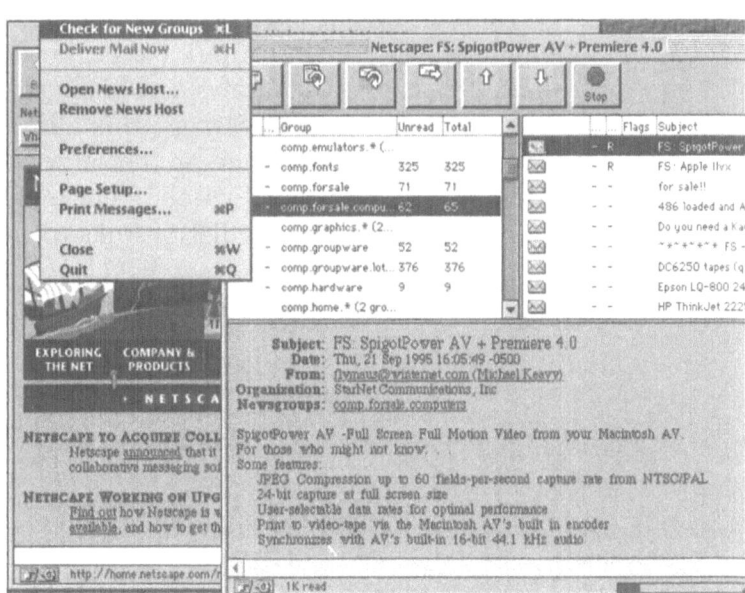

FIGURE 2.7.
Netscape 2.0's
News reader.

menus for opening bookmark files and creating new menus. You can now drag and drop bookmark links in the hierarchical list as well. Also, look for a button in the Show History panel you can use to place bookmarks directly.

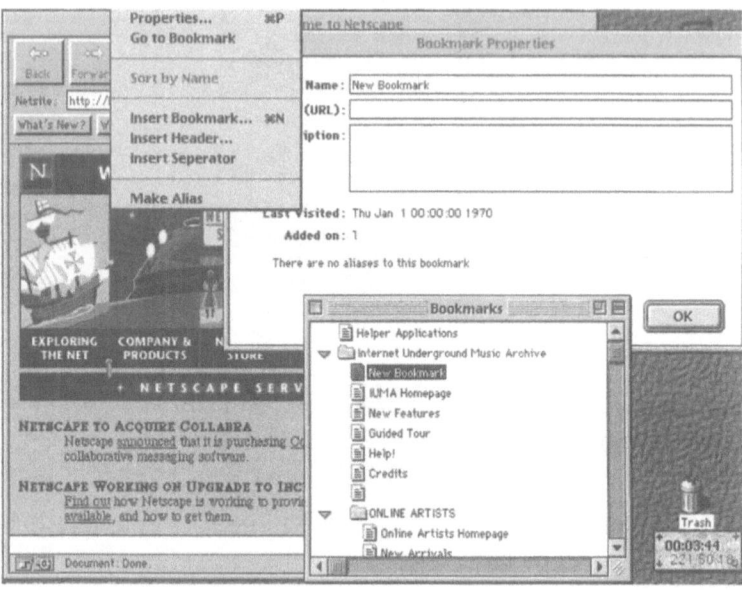

FIGURE 2.8.
Netscape 2.0's
Bookmarks system.

You'll find some of the more dramatic 2.0 improvements in its handling of new Web information types and structures, including frames. Netscape now allows scrolling regions to be placed in several areas inside a Web page; this allows information to be placed in separate containers in the same page.

There's also a much better Document Information panel in the 2.0 release that includes a list of links to the elements inside a document (like pictures and text files), as well as a more complete synopsis of the Web document.

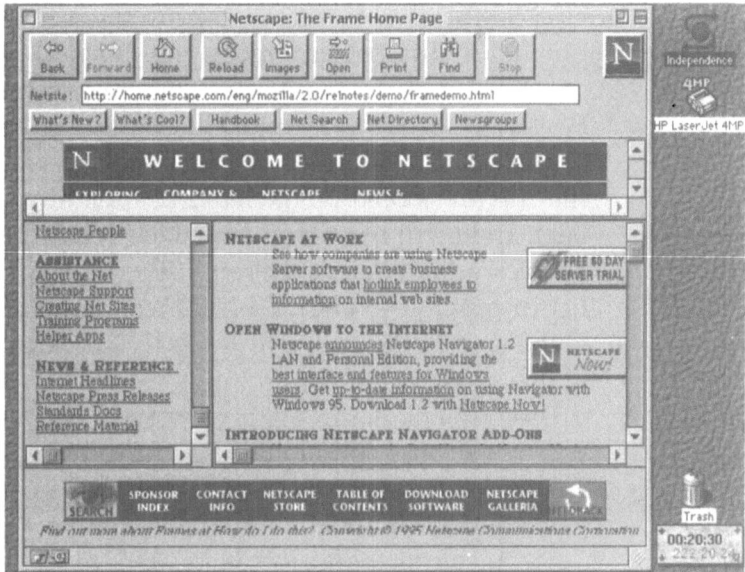

FIGURE 2.9.
A document using frames under Netscape 2.0.

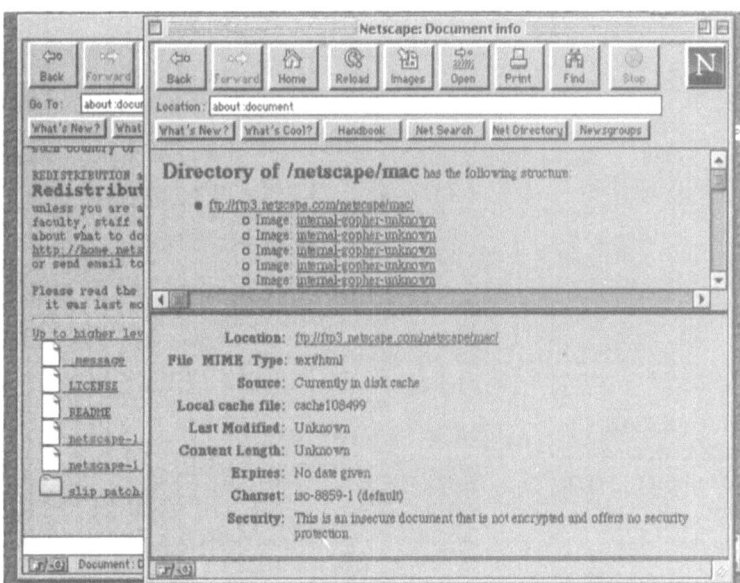

FIGURE 2.10.
The Document Information panel under Netscape 2.0.

NCSA Mosaic for Macintosh

NCSA Mosaic is a free Web browser from the National Center for Supercomputer Applications. It's still in development, and will continue to be updated. The current version is available as PowerPC native and standard Macintosh (68K) applications.

The main window shows the standard Web document view. At the top are icons for navigation, including buttons for moving back and forth between Web pages, loading default home pages, and reloading Web documents. There's also a drop-down history list of previously visited Web sites you can scroll through. The globe icon at the top right spins to indicate a document transfer in progress.

Directly below the main window is the URL panel, on which you can see the actual address of the Web document that you're viewing. You can also type an address in here directly, or cut and paste one to and from another document.

The program status line is located under the URL panel, and it shows link address information, document transfer status messages, and downloading information.

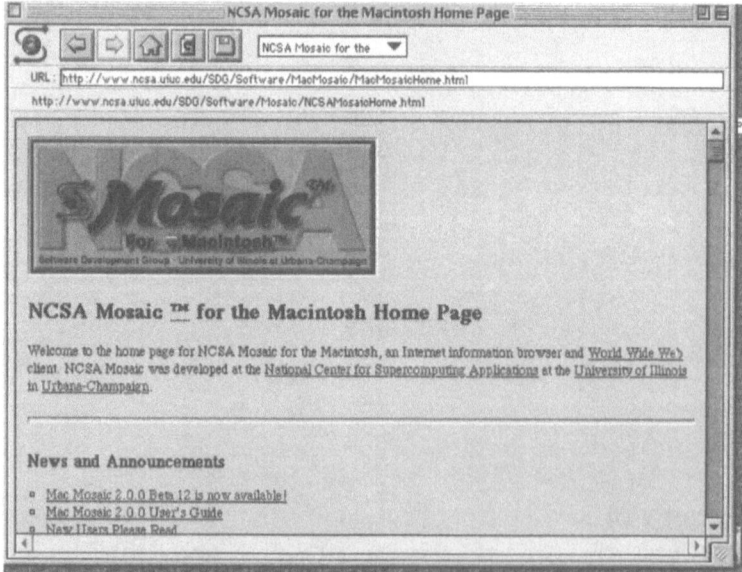

FIGURE 2.11.
NCSA Mosaic for Macintosh 2.0.0 Beta 12 main window view.

NCSA Mosaic's File Menu has standard items for opening a connection to a new URL (where you can specify a new Web site address), loading a local file, and reloading a current Web document. You can also spawn a new window and print from here. The File menu also features a View Source command that launches an external viewer to display a document's HTML source code (you may have to configure this to use a word processing application you already have, under the Options/Preferences/Helper Applications section for HTML—text/html). (See Figure 2.12.)

The Edit menu features Cut, Copy and Paste commands, and an undo item. You can use these with highlighted text from the main Web document window to move selections between applications. There's also a Show Clipboard command that will let you see what's currently in the clipboard, and a Find command that will let you search for text in the Web document currently loaded.

You can use the Options menu to hide the URL location and status message lines. This will increase the viewing area in your main browser window. This menu is where you'll also find items for resetting your home page, turning off automatic image loading, and switching on load to disk mode (for downloading files). There are also commands for flushing the local Web document cache and clearing out temp files that Mosaic may have created, to help you manage the amount of disk space the application will use. The Preferences item leads to a panel on which you can configure Mosaic, with sections for Miscellaneous preferences (default home page, Email address, and background colors), Links (where you can set link colors), Directories (for temp and hotlist directory settings), Gates (not the Microsoft guy, but where you'll configure your Usenet News and Mail servers), Apps (for setting up helper applications and adding new data types to Mosaic— you can review the default settings from here as well to see which applications Mosaic already knows about), and Cache (for turning the disk cache on and off, and for setting the maximum size and default cache directory).

The Style section under the Options menu can be used to change the overall look of Web documents in your Web browser. You can increase the font size, for example, or change paragraph spacing. There are also settings that will change the way tables and images are displayed. You shouldn't have to make changes in this section in most cases, because the results may not show

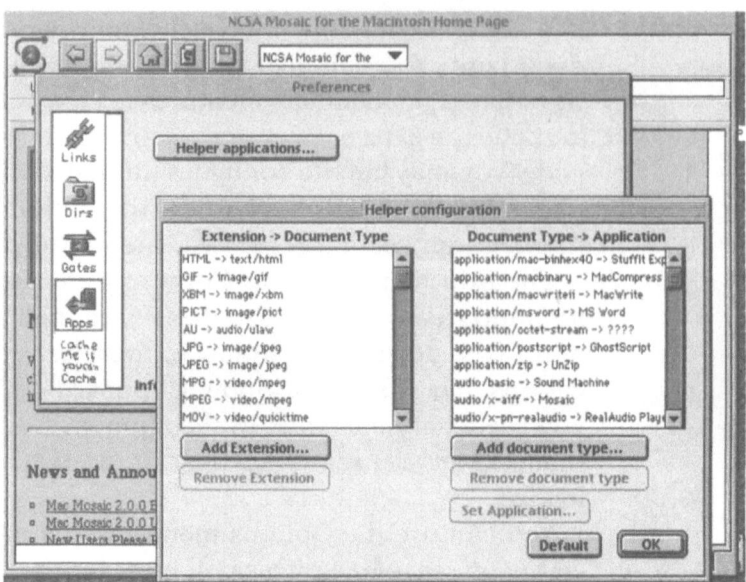

FIGURE 2.12.
Options/Preferences panels under NCSA Mosaic.

up well between different Web sites. There's a Default button that will reset the base styles in case you need to get back to standard settings.

The final item under the Options menu is for placing Mosaic into Kiosk mode. This changes the menus to remove most of the functions for configuring the program, and is most suitable to use when you don't want other users changing your settings.

The Navigation menu has commands for moving forward and back between documents, and for loading the default home page. There are also commands for bringing up the hotlist panel (on which you can manage multiple lists) and for adding documents to the current list. The Custom Menu item is a handy feature that lets you add your own menu of Web sites to Mosaic's top menu bar. You can also add current URLs to it, and attach hotlists.

Also in the Navigate menu are direct links to various Internet resources for further Net exploration. The Network Resources Meta Index is a good site for seeing the different types of information available over the Internet. There's also a link to the NCSA Mosaic for Macintosh Home Page here, so you can always reach it directly.

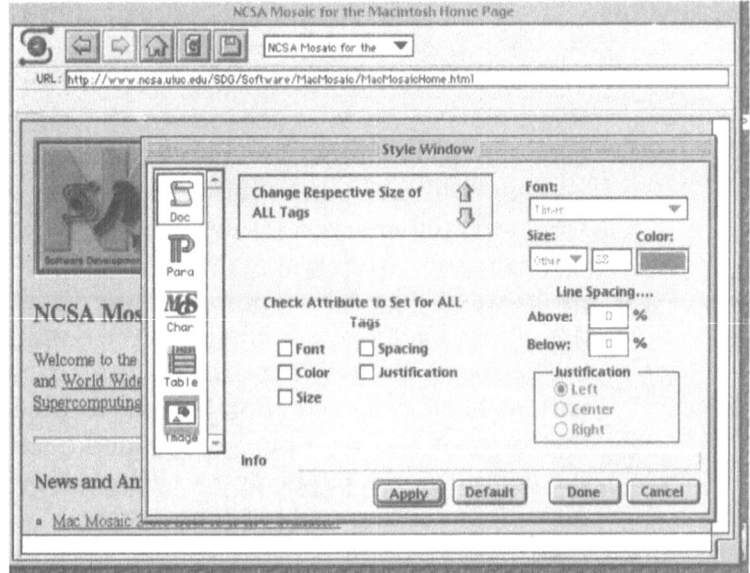

FIGURE 2.13.
Options/Styles
panel under NCSA
Mosaic.

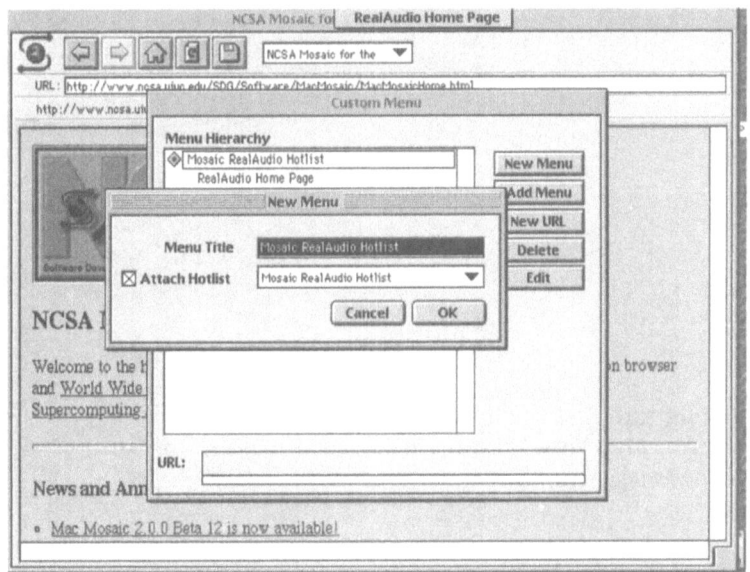

FIGURE 2.14.
The
Navigate/Custom
Menu panel under
NCSA Mosaic.

MacWeb

TradeWave's MacWeb (formerly from EINet) is a part of the Trade-
Wave Galaxy, an Internet index and search tool. The MacWeb
browser is currently moving toward a commercial release, but
you can still find a beta version available over the Internet and
from selected sources. It's available in PowerPC Native and 68K
Mac versions. TradeWave plans to add more of the features found
in browsers like Netscape (including in-line JPEG images and
document background effects) to the commercial release.

The main window features a standard Web document view,
with a short series of action buttons located at the top (for moving forward and back through loaded documents and reaching
the default home page), and a URL panel you can use to view a
document's actual address (and to type in a new one).

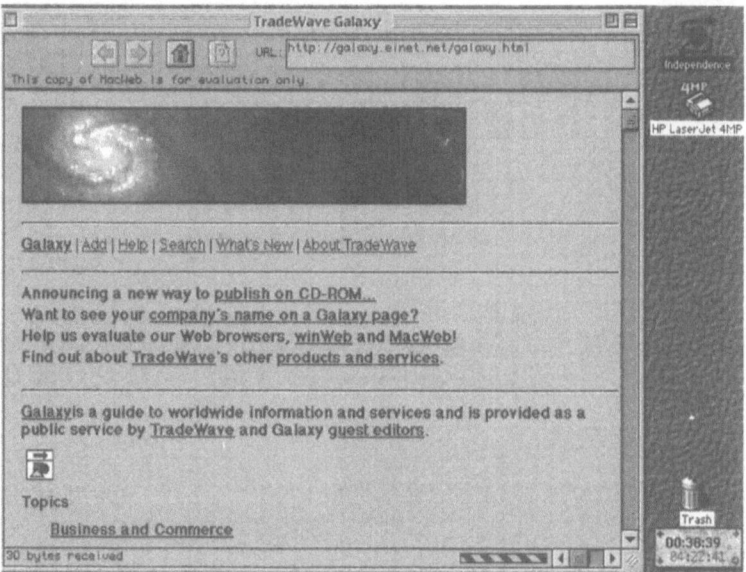

FIGURE 2.15.
MacWeb Main View
at the Galaxy Web
site.

Below the main window, there's a small progress indicator located to the bottom right and an area for status messages to the
left.

The File menu features items for launching a new main window, opening URLs (Web site addresses) and local files, and
printing. You can also save a URL from a document from here.
The File/Preferences menu item launches the main configura-

tion panels for MacWeb. These include categories for General settings (where you can enter an alternate home page address, and set up your Email address and Usenet News host), File and Folders (for setting up a specific folder for temporary files, and to specify a hotlist to launch at startup—an interesting feature), and Format (where you can set images to load automatically and change the default window background color).

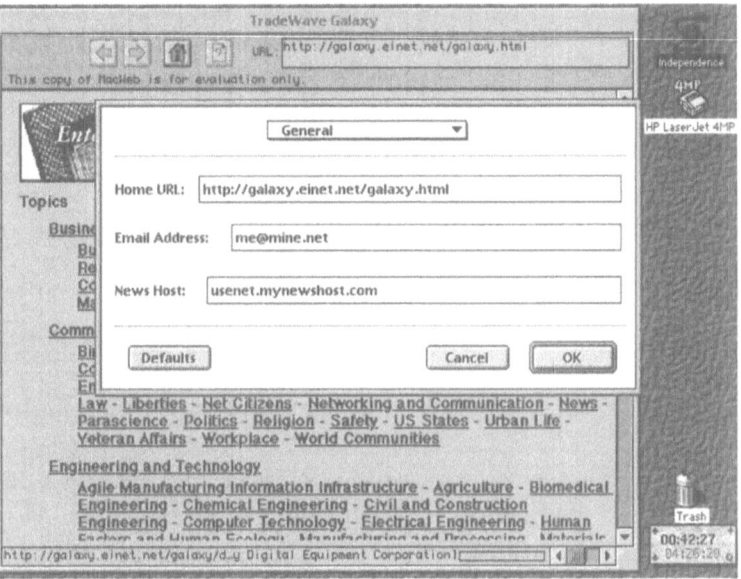

FIGURE 2.16.
MacWeb's
Preferences panel.

The Edit menu contains the standard Cut, Copy, and Paste features and Find functions (for searching through local documents). Below these items are more configuration settings panels for changing different HTML styles, setting helper applications, and adding new data type extensions. The Styles panel can be used to alter the way a Web document looks, by overriding the default HTML attributes. You can increase the font size for the main body text or change link colors, for example. Use these settings with caution, however, as making an incorrect choice could make Web documents fairly incomprehensible. There's a default button that will reset the system, fortunately. The Helpers panel shows the different data types MacWeb can recognize, and the default applications that they are set up to work with. You can change and add applications to the list from here as well. The Suffix settings specify the way MacWeb recognizes a data type by the filename extension. You can add new file suffix types to a data type by selecting one from a scrolling panel, and typing in the new suffix.

The Options menu has commands to load deferred images, and to view HTML source code (using SimpleText or an alternate word processor as a viewer). The Navigate menu has command equivalents for the forward and back buttons (used to move between documents) and for reaching the default home page, as well as a nested History menu you can scroll through to reach previously visited pages. There are also direct links to the Trade-Wave and MacWeb home pages you can use to get information on the current MacWeb releases.

The Hotlist menu for MacWeb allows you to add current documents to the menu itself. There are also functions for loading alternate hotlists and editing entry names and addresses.

PLUS Mosaic (Spyglass Enhanced NCSA Mosaic)

PLUS Mosaic is White Pine's version of Enhanced NCSA Mosaic. The Spyglass company licenses MacMosaic source code to commercial vendors, who produce versions with advanced features as part of their product offerings. PLUS Mosaic is a good example of how sophisticated versions of Enhanced NCSA Mosaic are becoming.

The main window shows the general Web document view. At the top of the window is a Toolbar with a good set of functions, including commands for loading a default home page, opening a URL or a local file, and reloading a document. You can also access local search functions from here. There are also commands for printing and saving documents. The hotlist button brings up a panel with favorite sites listed, where you can go to them directly and edit document names and addresses in the list. The Help system (available under the question mark) is integrated locally in HTML format, meaning you can use it without having to be connected to the Internet. It gives a good tutorial on how to use the program's many functions, with in-line images of the various program elements.

Below the Toolbar to the left are buttons for moving forward and back between Web documents, and a short progress bar that

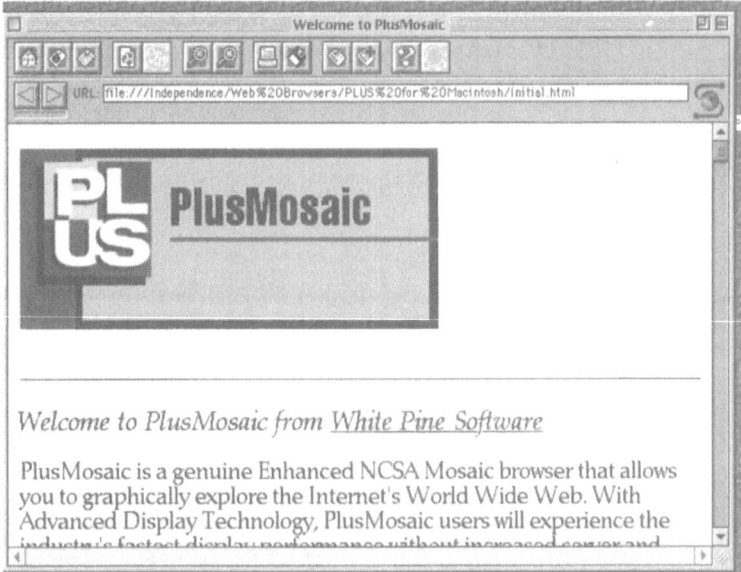

FIGURE 2.17.
PLUS Mosaic's main
window view.

will indicate the status of a document transfer. The spinning globe to the right is also a transfer indicator, but it spins at a constant rate and does not show how a transfer is progressing. Between these elements is the URL panel, which will show the Web address of the current document. You can also type in an address here to reach a Web site directly.

The File menu has standard commands for loading local files and URLs, spawning new windows, and printing. The Edit menu has the usual Cut, Copy and Paste commands for moving text from the Web document to other applications (and for pasting addresses into the URL panel), as well as a Find command (for searching the text in a Web document). The View Source command can be used to view the HTML code in the loaded document (using an independent viewer built into Enhanced Mosaic; you'll have to use keyboard commands to cut and copy text from here). Also located under the Edit menu is the command that loads the Preferences panel. Compared to other Web browsers, this is fairly straightforward. You can use it to turn off the Toolbar (to gain more space in the main viewing area) and to defer automatic image loading (for slow connections). There's also a place to specify your default home page and Usenet News server. The style sheet scrolling menu can be used to change the appearance of incoming Web documents (to increase overall font size, for example), but these styles are best used with caution, since they can seriously affect the way a document looks.

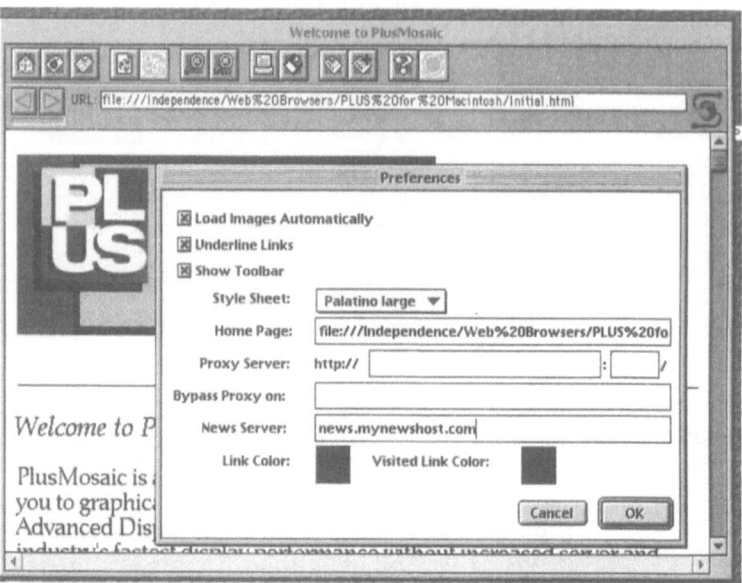

FIGURE 2.18.
PLUS Mosaic's
Preferences panel.

The Helpers menu item brings up a panel you can use to configure helper applications. By selecting a data type, the program can tell you if a helper applications has been configured for it, or if it has built-in support. PLUS Mosaic includes built-in support for in-line JPEG and GIF images, and also includes players for standard sound formats and QuickTime movies. You can also add new data types and helper applications quickly and easily here.

The Navigate menu had commands for moving forward and back between Web documents and for loading the default home page. You can also access the History panel from here. This shows a list of recently visited sites you can move to directly by clicking on their names. You can save the History list as an HTML file that you can then load into a browser (some browsers can also import this as a hotlist or bookmark file), an interesting way to save your Net surfing expeditions. PLUS Mosaic's hotlist panel (also under the Navigate menu) shows a basic list of sites that you can add to from the Navigate menu. You can edit the names and addresses of hotlist items from here, or export the hotlist file in HTML format.

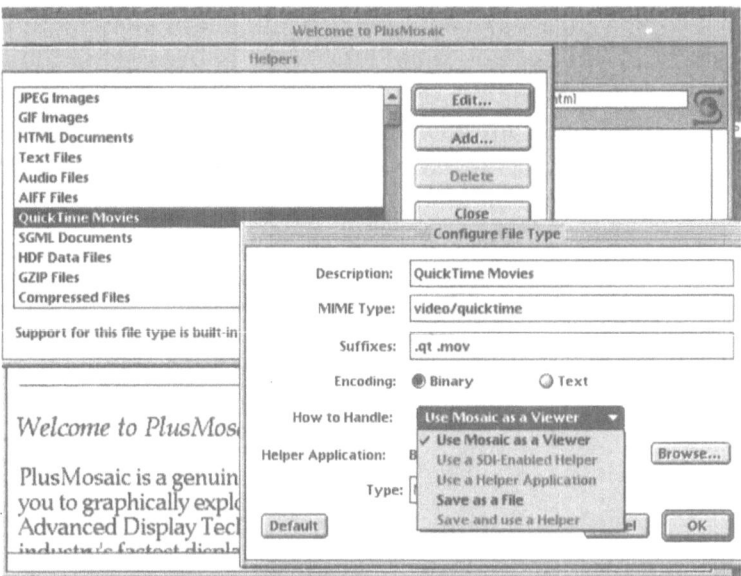

FIGURE 2.19.
PLUS Mosaic's
Helpers panel.

The Windows menu is designed to allow you to switch between different document windows quickly. It maintains a list you can scroll through of currently launched windows. You can also arrange multiple windows in a grid from here.

NetShark

NetShark is a browser that developed from Intercon's TCP/Connect II Internet connectivity software. It offers some good features, and shows that competition with Netscape can produce some interesting results.

The main NetShark window shows a standard Web page view, and the application also includes a floating button bar for common actions (like opening a local file or Web site connection, or launching the Hotlist panel). At the top of the main window there are also fixed buttons for moving between Web pages, reloading Web documents, and printing. Below these are panels that show the actual address of the Web page currently loaded, and the link address for a hyperlink in the document. To the right of these panels, a swimming shark fin shows that progression of a Web document transmission. Below that are a few buttons for accessing different services at the Netshark Web site, including a What's New directory, and a set of links to Internet search tools, and below these are two progress indicator bars that track Web page and image transfers. This can get a bit crowded, and you can use the Windows/Configuration panel to remove some of these elements (under the Web section). You might also want to move the button bar to the bottom of the main screen.

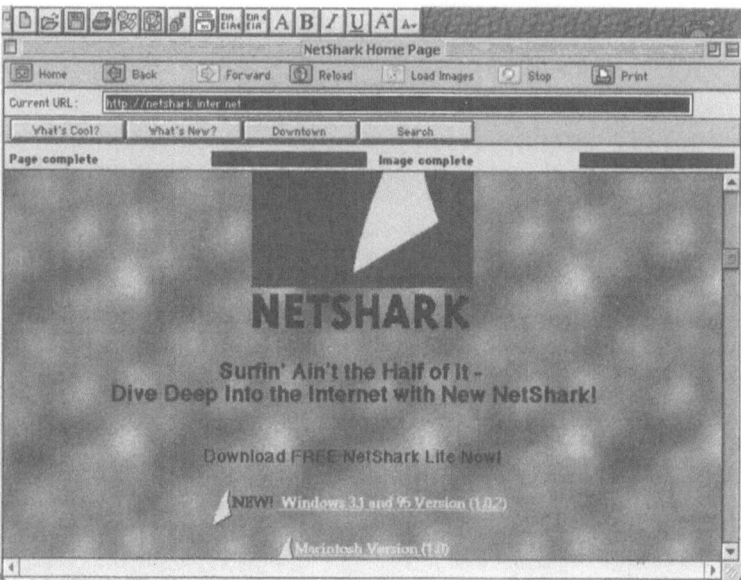

FIGURE 2.20.
Netshark's main window view.

The File menu has standard commands for opening local documents and printing, but you can also encode and decode Bin-Hexed files from here. The Edit menu has general Cut, Copy, and Paste commands, as well as the Find utility for searching through HTML documents.

Use the Web menu to open the Netshark home page or enter Web addresses (URLs). This menu lets you add the current document to the system Hotlist, and also launches the Hotlist panel. You can also bring up a Recent Items history panel from here. An HTML source viewer is built into Netshark, and you launch it from here. There are also switches you can use to turn off the Show URL and Show Link Location fields in the main window view, to give yourself more viewing area.

Netshark can also be used as an Email system. Once you're properly configured, you can use the Mailbox menu to check for new mail and access your local mailbox for stored messages.

Intercon was purchased by PSI, a large Internet Access Provider, and it's expected that they will more fully integrate their access accounts with this Web-based mail system. Ideally, it means that two Netshark users could send mail in Web format, complete with pictures and HTML formatting, across the Internet.

The Message menu works in conjunction with the Mail system to allow you to send messages with attachments directly from the Netshark browser. You also use this menu to extract attachments in messages you receive, and to play sound files. Use the Format menu to work with the Create Message panel to format your mail message with different font sizes and types, and to reformat paragraphs and quote from other messages.

Mail messages can also contain live hyperlinks to Web documents, and you can also set the system to check for mail automatically.

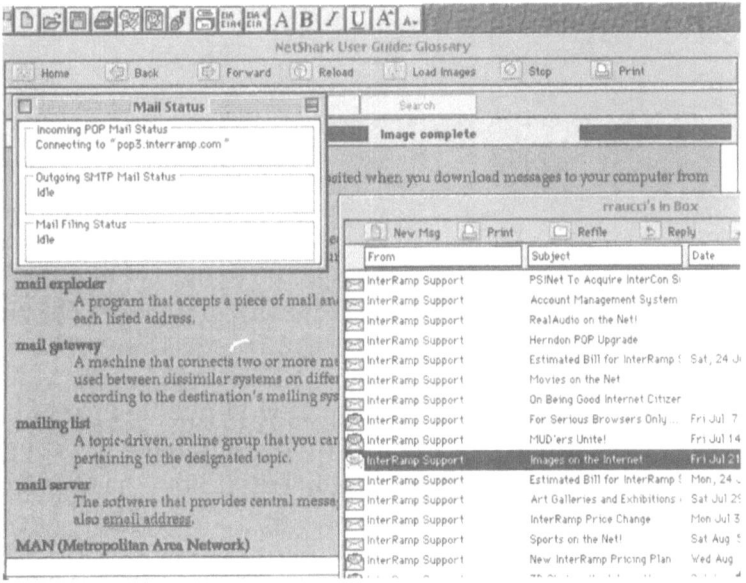

FIGURE 2.21.
Netshark's mail
capabilities.

The Windows menu under Netshark is where you'll configure the software. You can also show or hide your address book, a list of local mailboxes, a mail status panel, the Toolbar, and a general status panel.

Use the Configuration command to launch the NetShark Configuration panel. The first item is used to configure Mail. You'll want to set this up correctly with your Internet access provider to use NetShark's advanced mail capabilities. The Web section is where you'll set the default home page, and set colors for page links and text, and text size (you may not want to change these too much, as they can affect how every Web page will look). This section also allows you to switch off the URL and Link panels in the main window view, and to defer downloading images automatically. You can also set NetShark to launch a new window each time you jump to another URL.

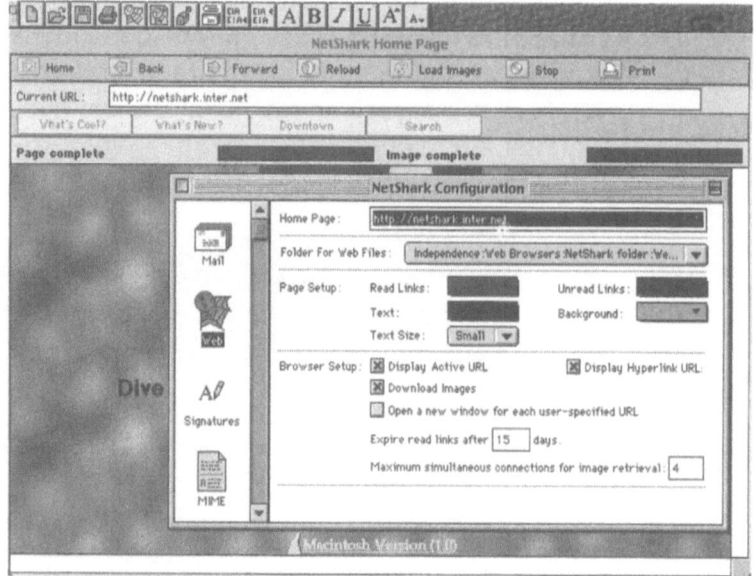

FIGURE 2.22.
NetShark's Windows/Configuration panel.

The Signatures section allows you to set up a signature file for Email. This is a short text tag that will be appended to the end of your Email messages. This is often used as a way to automatically add contact information to every message you send. Just type the signature you want into the open panel, and save it with a recognizable name.

The Mime section allows you to further set up how the page will look, and also allows you to turn off in-line viewing for the file formats that NetShark views directly (including GIF, JPEG, PICT, Mac sound files, and QuickTime). Use the Windows panel to turn off everything you don't need to view when NetShark starts up. You can also customize system alerts for mail functions from the Warnings configuration panel.

Helper Applications

Netscape and other Web browsers for Macintosh can display a variety of file formats directly in their main view windows, but not everything. Some graphics file formats and all sound files must be accessed via external programs called helper applications.

Netscape currently handles in-line .GIF and .JPG files well, so you don't need to install an external viewer for these picture formats. These are also the most common formats for Web pages. Some browsers may not support in-line .JPG images yet, so you'll have to configure an external program for them. Other image file formats (like .TIFF and PostScript) will also require you to configure an external program that can handle these, even with Netscape. Use the JPEGView shareware program as an external viewer. Version 3.3 can handle most file formats, including .GIF, .JPG, .TIFF, .BMP, MacPaint, and PICT.

Netscape and other Web browsers also need a player to be configured to use sound files on the Web properly (except Enhanced NSCA Mosaic, which has a player built-in). You can use the SimplePlayer application from Apple, or a shareware program like SoundMachine. Certain sites now support RealAudio, a software system that plays audio files as they download, instead of waiting for them to download first. You have to have the RealAudio application installed before you can access these files.

You'll also need certain players for motion video formats. In System 7.5, both the QuickTime Extension and a basic player (SimpleText) are already included (aren't you glad you got a Mac?), and Netscape will run QuickTime files automatically. You can also use the Sparkle shareware player to view QuickTime, MPEG video, and .AVI (Video for Windows) files. It features more comprehensive controls over movie playback.

You should also consider installing the free Adobe Acrobat Reader as an external helper application. This will allow Netscape and other browsers to view .PDF files will full text and image formatting. Some browsers will support Acrobat directly in their later releases; both Spyglass and Netscape have announced their intentions to add support for Acrobat formats internally, for example.

How to Add Helper Applications

Netscape gives you a number of easy ways to add helper applications. You should first look at the Preferences panel under the Options menu. Scroll down to the Helper Applications section, and you'll see a list of Mime types that Netscape can recognize, and the applications it will use to view them. A Mime type is a file format; for example, Netscape sees a GIF file as a Mime type of image/gif, and the action it performs is to load these types internally. The corresponding line in the Preferences panel shows this information, and allows you to change the applications and actions for a Mime type, or to add a new one. Note that the Internal option overrides the application setting; even though JPEGView is set as the application to use for GIF files, Netscape will view them in-line instead.

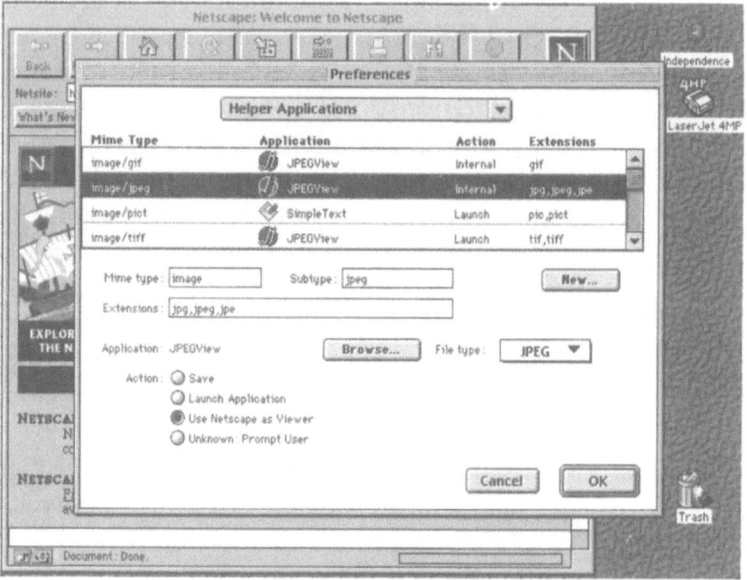

FIGURE 2.23.
Netscape's Helper
Applications
Preferences panel.

Scroll through the Helper Applications list to see which programs your version of Netscape is preconfigured to use. This will give you a good idea of which programs to get via FTP from Mac shareware directories. You can use any application you want to view Web Mime types, according to the system and software you have; just make sure the programs you use can handle the file types specified.

You can also look at Netscape's Macintosh Helper Applications page at their home page (under the Assistance/ Helper Apps section). This gives a good set of links to archive sites for Mac helper applications, and also has links to annotated file archives for some of the different programs.

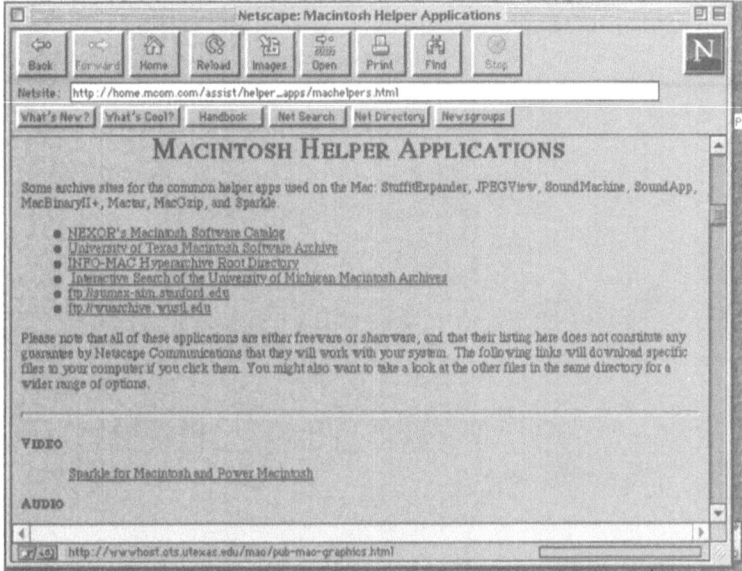

FIGURE 2.24.
Netscape's Macintosh Helper Applications page.

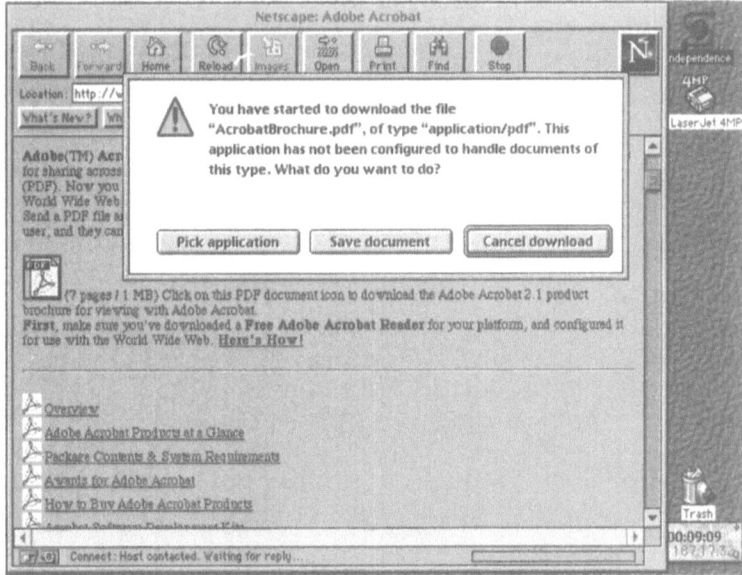

FIGURE 2.25.
Netscape's automatic helper application configuration system.

Netscape can also configure helpers directly after it encounters a new Mime type for the first time. When Netscape sees a type of file it's not configured for, it will ask you if you want to save it to disk (to use with an off-line reader), or pick an application to use. After you select Pick Application, you can then browse for the application you want to use to view these types of files. For our example, we've clicked on a link to an Acrobat .PDF file, and will use the resultant dialog box to pick the Acrobat Reader program we've previously installed. (See Figure 2.25 on page 47.)

3
The Access Provider

Choosing an access provider is the most important step you'll take in running Netscape and other Web browsers. There are a number of different types of service providers that give access to the Internet. First, we'll look at a shell account.

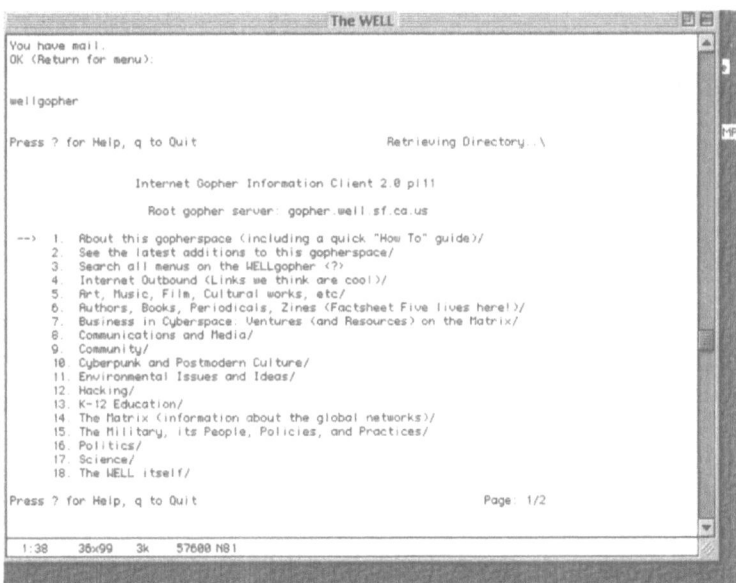

FIGURE 3.1.
A shell account on the WELL in Sausalito.

The shell account is an indirect connection to the Internet. This means that what you actually get when you connect to your service provider via modem is a session running on the remote system, not your computer. Depending on the programs available on the remote system itself, this account may have a wide range of Internet capability, but it won't be able to run Netscape, and the Internet access programs will be text-based, and will not work like standard Mac applications.

This is because Netscape runs as a client program. The information it uses needs to load directly into it on your local system, not on a remote system.

A shell account uses a store and forward method of transaction. Your shell account usually gives you a personal file directory on the remote system. When you use FTP (File Transfer Protocol) to transmit a file from a remote site, it comes to your directory on the remote computer, not directly to your local system. You then have to download it from that system to yours.

Netscape uses a method of transaction known as TCP/IP (Transfer Control Protocol/Internet Protocol) to pass information directly from computers on the Internet to itself. These protocols were originally designed for high-speed computer networks, but versions were subsequently developed that could run over standard telephone lines. SLIP (Serial Line Internet Protocol) and PPP—indexPPP (Point-to-Point Protocol) are terms for types of access to the Internet that standard modems and ISDN equipment can use to run graphical interface programs like Netscape.

There's more to it than that, however. The shell type of account usually provides you with some kind of actual service organization, whereas the SLIP and PPP types of accounts bring the Internet connection right down to your own system, and often leave you there. That's because the shell account runs on a remote computer system, while the SLIP/PPP provider is more of a gateway right down to your system.

Selecting an Internet access provider with a proper level of support is crucial. An example provider is the WELL (The Whole Earth Lectronic Link), of Sausalito, California (at `http://www.well.com`). The WELL originally started as a shell Internet account provider (which is still a main part of the service it offers), but also now provides the Whole Works Internet Toolkit, a series of Internet applications that also includes a dial-up connection to the Internet, the software you need to make the connection, and a WELL membership. The Toolkit also installs the latest version of Netscape Navigator.

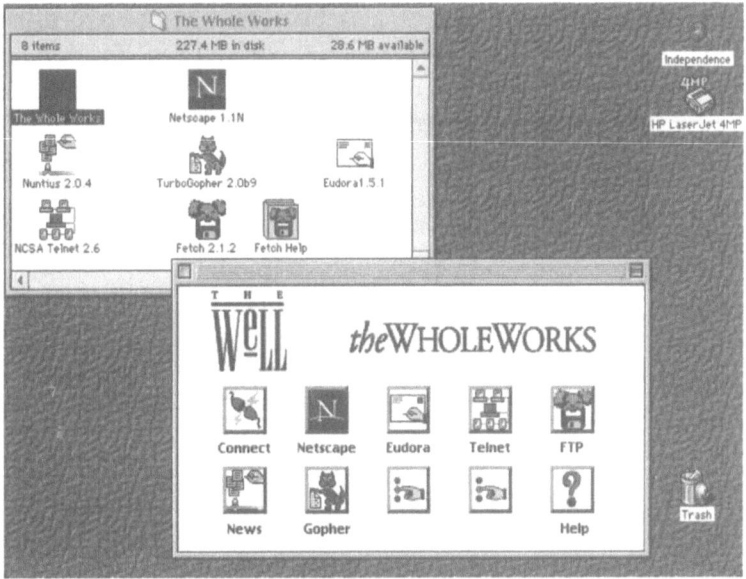

FIGURE 3.2.
The Whole Works
WELL application
and software folder.

Prices for Internet access vary, but expect to pay about $29/ month for 29 hours of connect time, and then $1–2 per hour after that. There are Internet access providers with lower bulk rates, but make sure they have fast connection equipment (i.e., their modems should be as least as fast as yours), and can provide you with connection software (or at least give you the tech support you'll need to configure the software you can get on your own).

You can find Internet access providers listed in computer magazines and newspapers. It's important to note that on-line services like EWorld and America Online are not true Internet access providers yet; they may offer a limited form of Internet access, but don't expect them to run a Web browser like Netscape with the same functionality of a standard access provider account (though AOL is planning to offer this type of service in the future). A stand-alone PPP account is still your best bet for full access. You should also be able to configure your Mac Internet connection software (MacTCP and MacPPP) for different access providers fairly easily, meaning that you can switch between service providers if you find a better deal. Also note that service providers like the WELL will have preconfigured MacTCP and MacPPP software as a part of their software packages and connection plans.

You may also want to look to the future when you're choosing an Internet access provider. Some are already including ISDN connection service as well as fast modem access. For example, PSI (Performance Systems International) offers a Mac connection software package with their Internet access accounts, and their service works with fast modems and ISDN equipment. PSI's Mac package also includes standard Internet access tools.

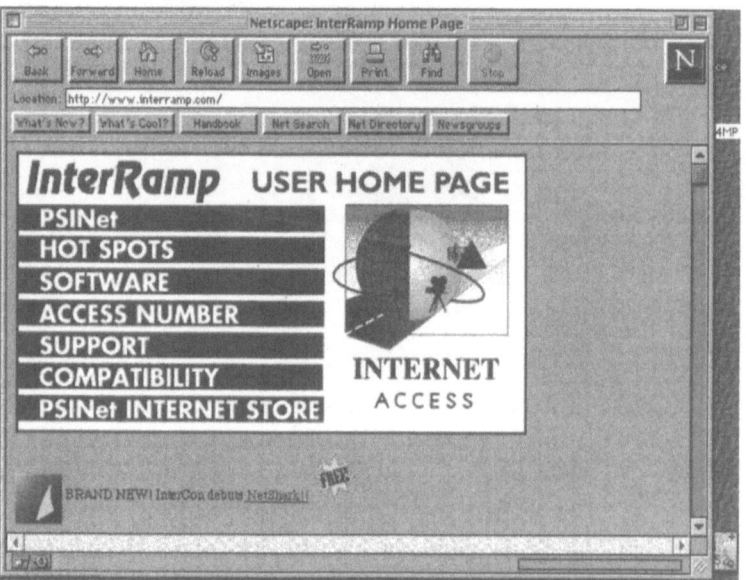

FIGURE 3.3.
PSI's Web site.

You can get a trial version of PSI Instant Interamp Internet connection software at PSI's Web site. This software will configure a PSI dial-up account for you. You can also reach the software via FTP at ftp.psi.com in the /iiramp/intercon directory.

Apple also has a full Internet package, called the Internet Connection Kit. This includes the Apple Internet Dialer application that gets you connected quickly with preconfigured Internet system software, a set of helper applications that includes Acrobat Reader, and a fully licensed version of Netscape. Find out more about it from your Apple dealer, or at http://www.apple.com.

MacTCP and MacPPP

Most access providers that sell a Mac Internet connectivity package will provide you with the two crucial parts for your Internet connection (MacTCP and MacPPP). It's also possible to get this software on your own. MacTCP is the basic Internet connection Control Panel you'll use to move information across the World Wide Web to your Macintosh. It's a standard part of System 7.5.

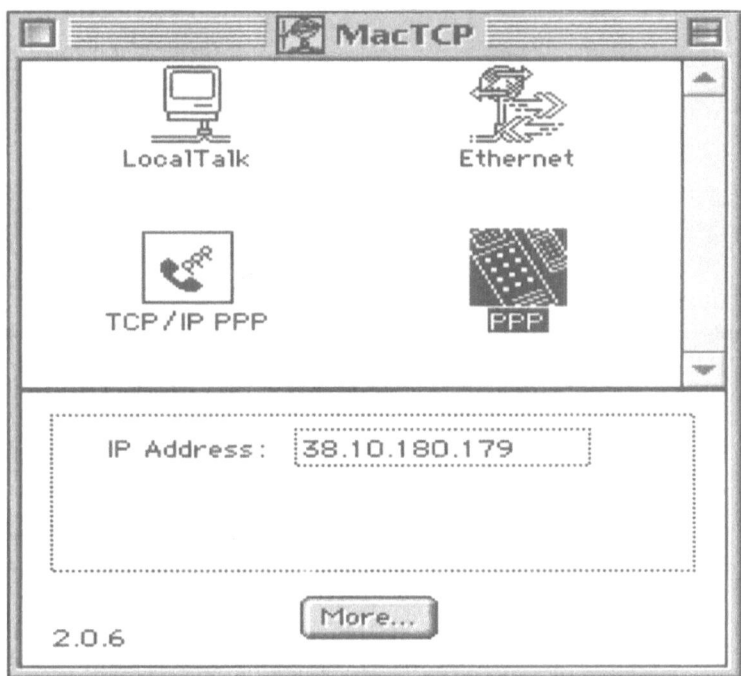

FIGURE 3.4.
MacTCP Control
Panel.

The TCP/IP protocol was originally designed for high-speed Ethernet networks, but has been adapted for modem use by using a software protocol called PPP. The second part of your Mac Internet connection is therefore MacPPP, a software package that includes the PPP extension and the ConfigPPP Control Panel. You can find it at selected shareware sites or vendors or from a service like BMUG (Bay Area Mac Users' Group, http://www.bmug.org).

Once you place the PPP extension into the proper folder (just drop it on the System Folder, and the Mac operating system will take it from there), you'll be able to configure MacTCP to use PPP. From the MacTCP Control Panel, highlight the PPP icon (it supposedly shows two telephones, but it looks more like a pair of Band-Aids), and click on the More button. You'll see the MacTCP configuration screen for your PPP connection.

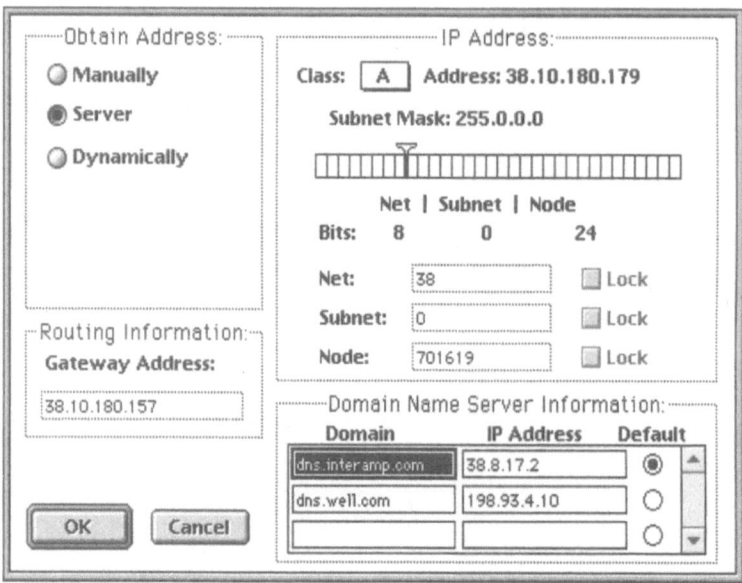

FIGURE 3.5.
MacTCP PPP
configuration
screen.

This panel includes information that allows Netscape to find Web addresses through a system called Domain Name Resolution. When you enter a Web site address (for example, www.apple. com), or click on a site link, MacTCP passes the request from Netscape to your Internet access provider's DNS system, and back to you (via PPP). The DNS system resolves the address and finds it, which allows Netscape to make the connection and receive the site information. You'll add the DNS server name and address number from your access provider, as well as gateway information (the Internet path to your access provider). Some providers will already configure this panel for you, as a part of their startup packages. You'll only have to change this panel if you switch access providers, or if you're configuring it by yourself.

The next part of your Mac Internet connection is the ConfigPPP Control Panel. This panel is used to make your modem connection to your access provider. The main window shows status icons (versions 2.04 to 2.1 PPP DOWN, two unhappy disconnected faces, PPP UP, two happy connected faces; version 2.2, a

handshake or released hands) and buttons for opening and closing the connection, and for reading connection statistics. The 2.2
release has some different settings and icons and shows connection rate information when you make your connection, but is
relatively similar to the 2.04 and 2.1 releases (it incorporates the
overall major changes, however). Both versions also have short
pull-down menus for choosing which serial port to use (modem
or printer), and setting the idle timeout and echo intervals. You
probably won't need to change the latter two settings; just make
sure you have ConfigPPP connected to the same serial port as
your modem.

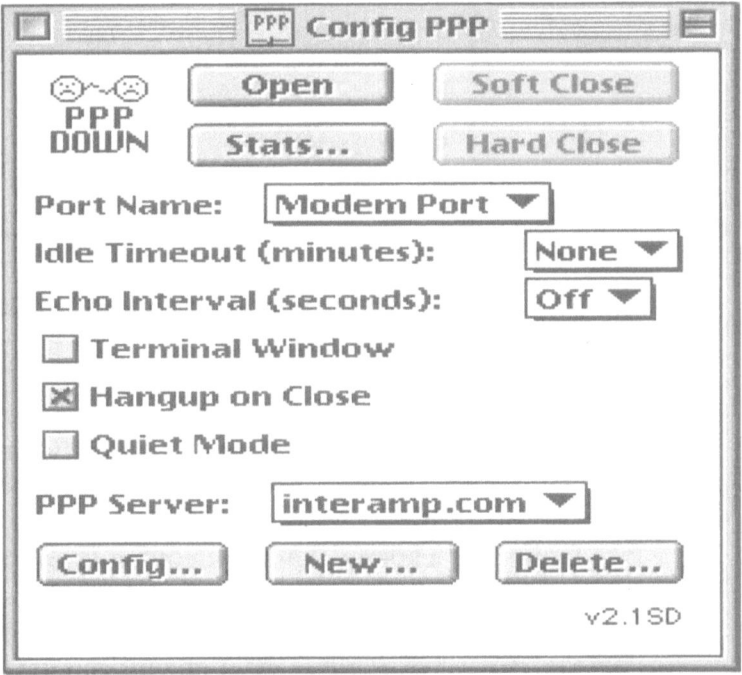

FIGURE 3.6.
ConfigPPP 2.1SD
main screen.

   Below these menus are switch boxes for setting up a terminal
window, automatically hanging up on closing your connection,
and for entering quiet mode. You shouldn't need the terminal
window to be set for a general PPP connection, unless you're
very comfortable with making your connections manually. On
the other hand, you should set ConfigPPP to automatically hang
up on close to make sure your connection has been fully broken
(remember, connect time is money!). Quiet mode is up to you;

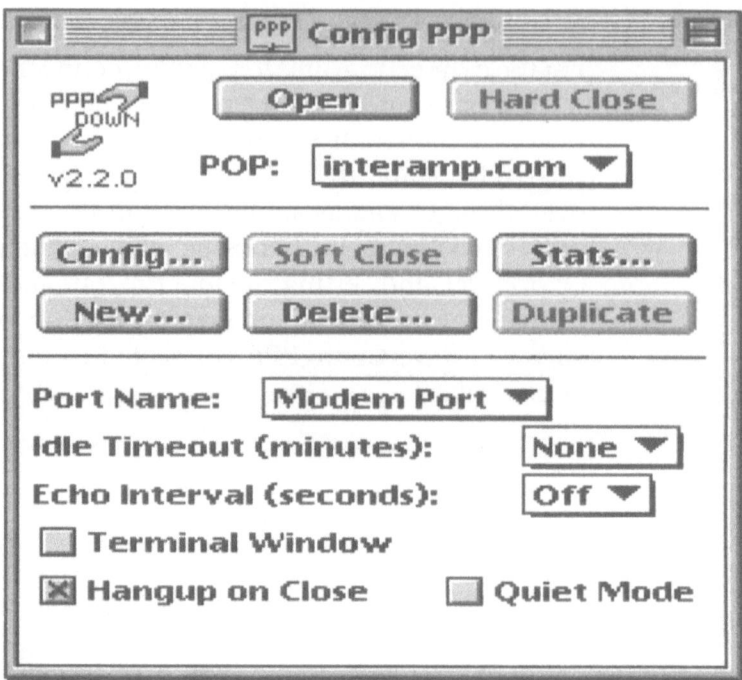

FIGURE 3.7.
ConfigPPP 2.2 main
screen.

you can avoid the screeching modem connect sounds if you like.

The PPP Server menu is a scrolling list you can use to keep multiple access provider profiles set up to work with MacPPP. Your access provider server name should be set to appear in the default menu view. You can use the New and Delete buttons to set up and remove access provider PPP servers, which will then appear in or be removed from the PPP Server menu. The Config button leads to the main configuration screen for your PPP server.

This is where you'll configure your modem to work with PPP. You can select a port speed that will match your modem's highest transfer rate, set flow control (for CTS-DTR hardware handshaking, protocols designed to make modem transmissions more reliable), and specify modem Init strings you may need to use to set up your modem properly. There's also a place to enter in your access provider's default phone number. Make sure your provider can give you a local call number; otherwise, you may be adding long distance charges to your connect time charges. Change the Modem connect timeout settings only if your system seems to need more time to make a connection.

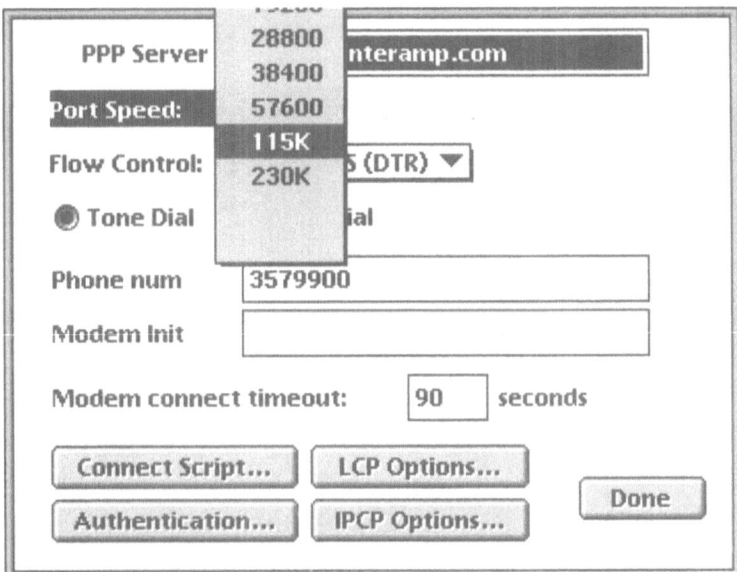

FIGURE 3.8.
ConfigPPP PPP
server main
configuration
screen.

Note: Most Macs have a maximum serial rate of 56K, due to their serial port chipset. Newer Macs (including the Quadra AV and PowerMac series) include a faster serial chip that can reach around 128K, suitable for use with some modems and ISDN equipment and access providers. Earlier versions of MacPPP can only be configured to 56K, however. You can look for altered versions of MacPPP like MacPPP 2.11SD (the initials stand for the person who did the alteration) on FTP sites like those available from `mirror.apple.com`. This version allows you to configure your modem port beyond 56K and can make some Macs achieve faster Internet connections.

The buttons at the bottom of the main configuration screen are used to set the basic access parameters of MacPPP and your Internet access provider account. These should only be set with information from your access provider. The Connect Script button leads to a panel that refers to an authentication process your system may go through with your access provider's server. (See Figures 3.9 and 3.10.)

The Wait setting means your system will wait for this information string to be received before proceeding; the Out setting means your system will transmit this information to the PPP server. You should be careful with this panel; you may be told to set it up to log in to your access provider by entering your

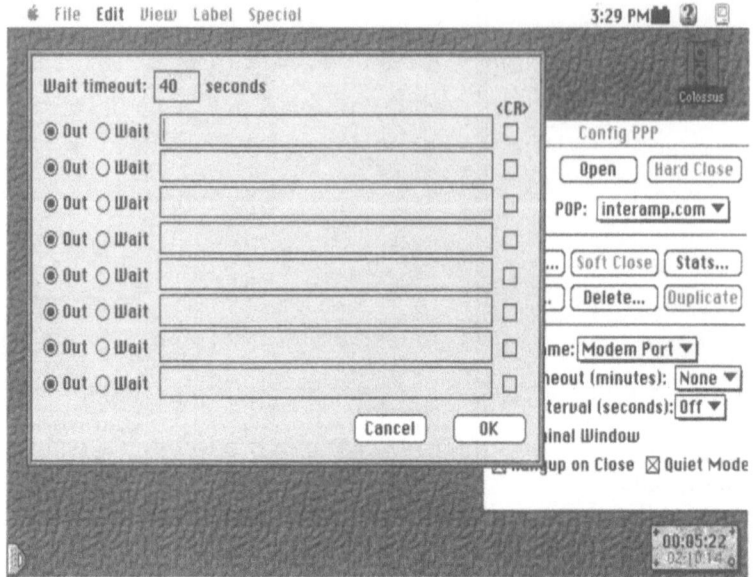

FIGURE 3.9.
Connect Script
panel in ConfigPPP.

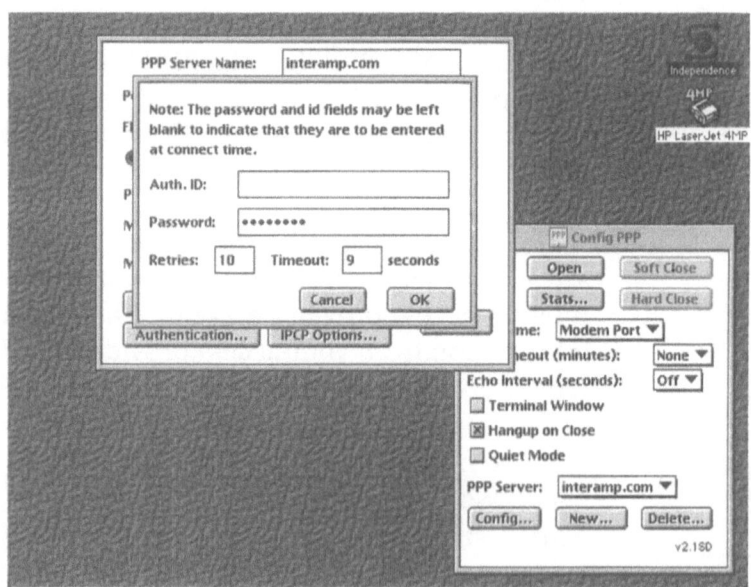

FIGURE 3.10.
Authentication panel
in ConfigPPP.

account name on one line and your password on another, but your password line is not encrypted and can be read by anyone who can launch the ConfigPPP control panel! Most Internet access provider accounts can bypass this panel entirely, and use a dynamic authorization process built into PPP (called PAP, Password Authentication Protocol). Make sure yours can.

The password field in the Authentication panel is encrypted, however, and this is where you'll add your main access provider Authorization ID as well. You may have to adjust the retry and timeout settings for your particular connection.

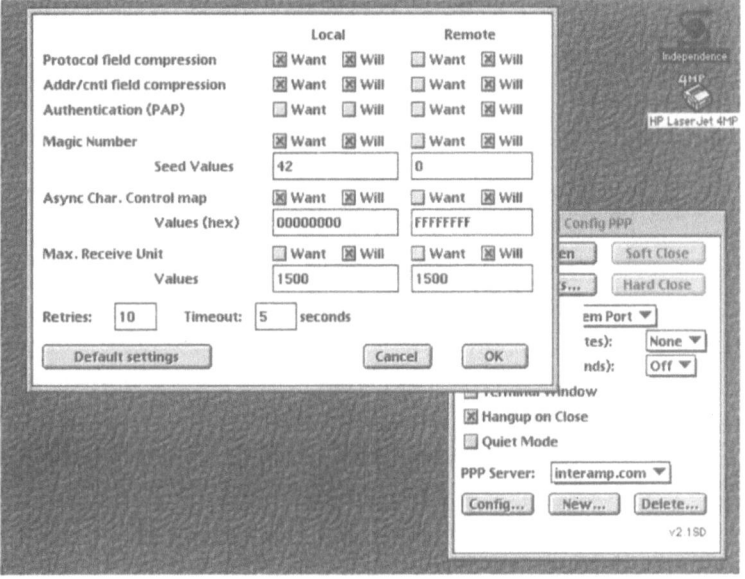

FIGURE 3.11.
LCP panel in ConfigPPP.

Use the LCP panel carefully. You'll need to have the various protocols and compression settings matched exactly to your access provider's PPP server settings, and you may have to tweak the retry and timeout settings to make this work as well. Once again, make sure your access provider can help you with this, or get a startup package including a version of MacPPP that is configured for your provider.

The same caveats go for the IPCP panel. The settings for TCP header compression and IP address specification should be set for your access provider server connection to work properly.

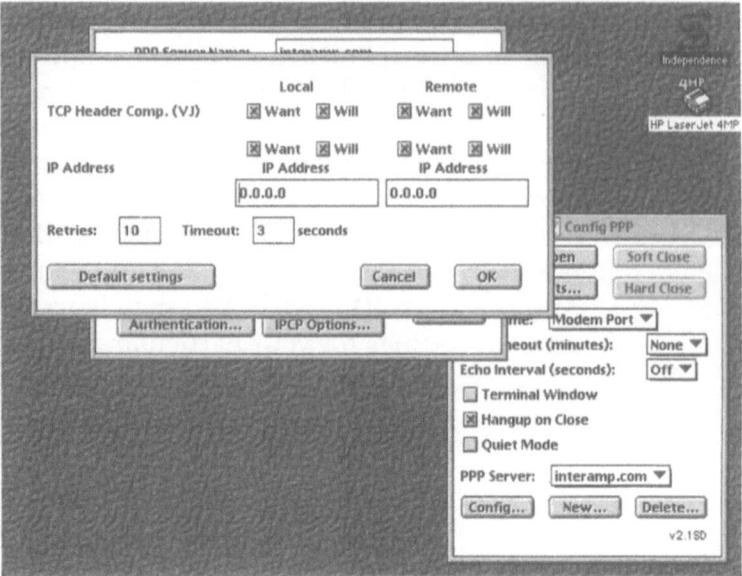

FIGURE 3.12.
IPCP panel in
ConfigPPP.

Running MACPPP

To run MacPPP, make sure you've got MacTCP properly set to use PPP. Then, launch the ConfigPPP Control Panel, and click on the Open button. You should see status screens indicating that the PPP system is dialing out through your modem, and messages indicating that the connection is taking place. The PPP DOWN icon will change to the PPP UP icon, and you're connected. Now you can start Netscape, and reach the World Wide Web. Netscape will also automatically launch MacPPP when you start it.

Remember that your connection is still up when you close the ConfigPPP Control Panel; you don't want to accidentally leave it up, since you'll continue to rack up connect time charges. Netscape also won't bring up the ConfigPPP Control Panel when it launches PPP automatically. You'll have to remember to bring it up yourself after you quit Netscape, or you'll stay connected. To close your connection, hit the Hard Close button; this will disconnect your modem. The Soft Close button is used to allow MacPPP to reopen automatically if another application needs TCP services. This could result in your system is re-establishing your PPP connection behind your back, leaving you liable for connect time charges. This can be especially troublesome since most applications and services run MacPPP in the background;

if they accidentally start it up, you may not even have any evidence that you have a connection running, and you'll have to open the ConfigPPP Control Panel to see if the connection is up. A Hard Close means that MacPPP will break your connection and be closed to other programs, and will only dial when you specifically trigger it.

There are useful utilities for keeping track of your PPP usage and showing your connect time progress. MacPPP Timer is a small application that can do both. It runs ConfigPPP in the background (like Netscape, it doesn't open the Control Panel, but you'll see the connection screens), and can automatically start a PPP session. Then, as the connection progresses, MacPPP Timer places a small panel directly below the Trashcan that shows the elapsed connect time. There's also a resettable display that shows your cumulative connect time, helpful for estimating your Internet service charges.

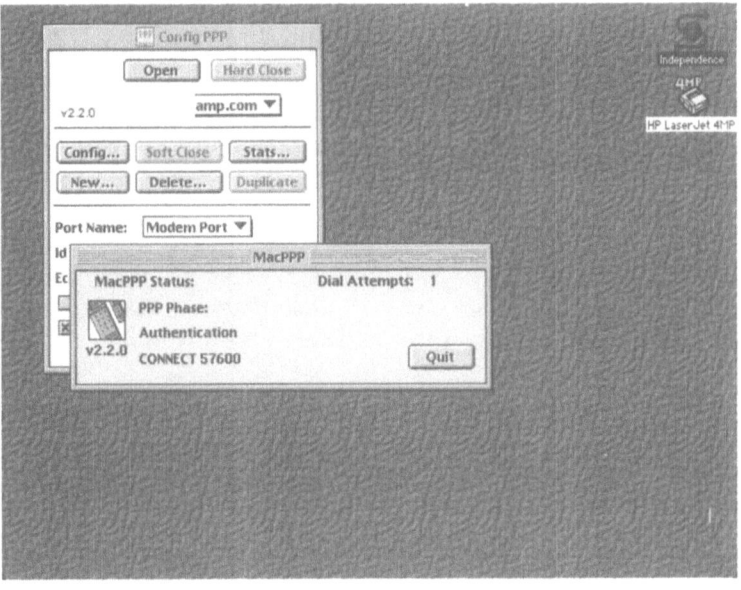

FIGURE 3.13.
The MacPPP 2.2
connection display
panel.

MacPPP Timer is easy to use. You can put an alias of the program in your Apple Menu, and launch it from there. The small display panel (in versions 1.3 and above) has a series of control "hot spots." These include two small switches on the left side; clicking on the lower red arrow will close the PPP connection, and clicking on the blue arrow will bring it back up. You can use these switches as an easy way to disconnect and reconnect your system without having to open the ConfigPPP Control Panel. The right-hand-side switches allow you to quit the program (the small Q symbol) or to launch the program's Preferences panel (the arrow pointing right).

The Preferences panel (also available from the File menu) allows you to set MacPPP Timer to automatically launch PPP when you start it (the preferred method), and switches to control the cumulative timer. You can also turn off the display panel's "hot spots."

FIGURE 3.14.
The MacPPP Timer display panel.

You can also start and end your PPP sessions from the File menu. Remember, starting Netscape first may automatically launch your PPP connection in the background, and this will bypass the PPP Timer. Always start MacPPP Timer before Netscape, and let it automatically make your PPP connection.

4
Modems and ISDN Adapters

Once you've got your access provider chosen and the Macintosh Internet connection software installed, the next thing to do is to connect via modem. This chapter covers modems and modem protocols, and internal vs. external modems. It also discusses standard and DMA-controlled (GeoPort) serial ports for ensuring trouble-free data communications. We then look at how ISDN is bringing even higher-speed digital connections to the desktop.

Choosing a modem is very important to running Netscape over a telephone line. It's important to note that Netscape needs the highest-speed connection you can get to your Internet access provider. The hardware you use is crucial for this. Netscape transfers pictures, sound, and program files directly to your system, and it takes a lot of speed to keep up with the information flow. A minimal modem speed can slow your transfers down and significantly degrade your Netscape experience. Get the fastest modem you can.

A 9600-baud modem is the bare minimum for running Netscape, and most versions suggest a 14.4K-baud speed. While a text-based Internet service can run on a 2400-baud modem, it's too slow for Netscape and Netscape's helper applications. Comparatively, a 14.4K baud modem is six times faster at transferring data. Access providers and modem companies are also working at ways to increase throughput via special data-compression techniques. These features, found on the latest 14.4K-baud modems, can increase their speeds to 19.2K , 28.8K, or even 57.6K baud. Accordingly, 28.8K modems can be twice as fast as that.

The increased speeds are factors of the efficiency of your Internet connection software as well as your modem. For example, the Config screen for MacPPP 2.01's ConfigPPP Control Panel allows you to select up to a 57.6K connection even with a 14.4K-baud modem. You may need a 28.8K-baud modem to make that speed possible, however.

Differences in your Internet access provider now play a part in the overall connection. The tradeoff lies in the best price/performance relative to speed. A 19.2K connection is adequate, but you should try for the highest connection you can get—57.6K if possible, or even higher.

The path is now as follows: modem to Internet access software to Internet access provider. The connection from the Mac to the modem is also very important, however.

A modem uses a UART (Universal Asynchronous Receive/Transmit) chip to process data. This chip is built into a Mac's standard serial ports, and also into internal modems. The UARTs built in to non-GeoPort Mac serial ports transfer information through the main system processor before passing it to memory. This can slow the rate information can flow through the system, and therefore slow down the rate at which you can connect to your access provider via modem. Apple recently introduced a DMA-controlled (direct memory access) serial port on advanced Macs (the Quadra AV 660/840, Centris 660AV, and all PowerMac desktops) that addresses this problem, and allows them to use GeoPort technology.

It's not going to be too noticeable in the near future; most Macs can achieve a high speed through their standard serial ports. You'll notice it mostly when you configure MacPPP. The ConfigPPP Config panel with a standard copy of MacPPP 2.01 will let you set the port speed only to 57.6K (near the maximum rate of non-DMA Macs). Quadra AV and PowerMac owners will have to use an altered copy of MacPPP designed for the DMA serial port Macs to get more choices in this menu, beyond 57.6K. Look

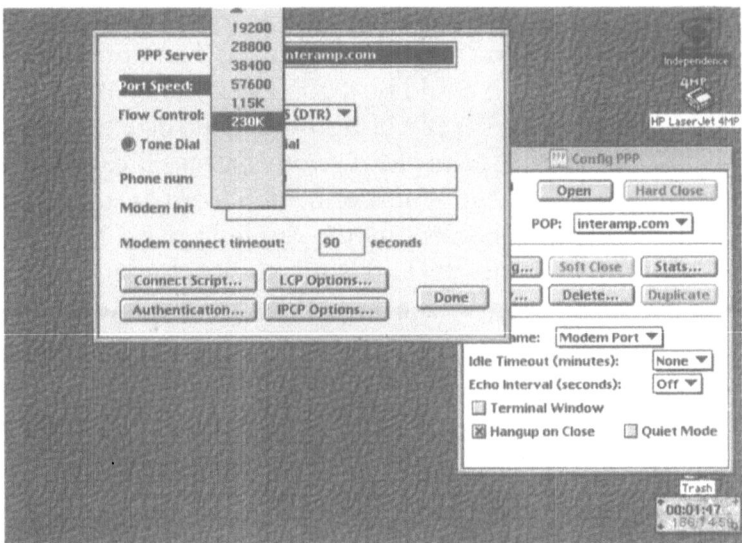

FIGURE 4.1.
MacPPP 2.2
ConfigPPP
configuration panel,
showing the Port
Speed menu.

for MacPPP 2.1SD to 2.2 and higher-numbered versions, available at Mac shareware sites.

To get the higher speed, you should check with your access provider to see if they can support it. Then make sure your own local modem can support it as well. You should then be able to select the higher speed from the MacPPP 2.1SD ConfigPPP Config panel for your access provider setup, and make the connection.

Modems and Geoport Telecom Adapters

Macs can use a wide range of modems, including low-cost PC external types. If you're using a PC-type modem with a PC serial connector (DB25; 25-pin to your Mac serial port) make sure you have the proper cable to connect to your Mac; you'll need one that supports hardware handshaking (not just a printer cable!). There are also modems designed specifically for Macintosh, including the Supra 14.4 External. These will usually come with the cables you need, and some will have them already attached to the modem. The Mac's good overall design also allows some of these modems to draw power from the system ADB port. You just plug them into both ports (and plug your keyboard/mouse into the back of the modem's ABD cable), and you're connected, with no external power support to worry about.

Powerbooks can use external modems of any sort, but you'll have to carry them around. The Supra 14.4 external Macintosh modem could be a good idea, since it doesn't require an external power supply of it's own. But the extra drain on your ADB port will certainly lower your battery life (not as much of a concern if you use it while connected to an AC outlet). Internal modems for Powerbooks include Apple Express Modems and Global Village PowerPorts, and both can be configured to run PPP. Use the 2.2 version of the MacPPP Control Panel, and select the Internal Modem option under the Port Name menu. Make sure you also have MacTCP installed properly.

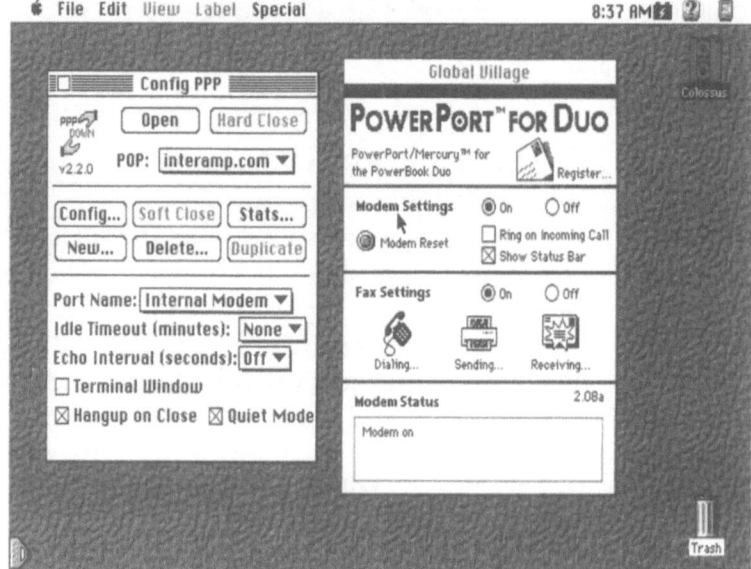

FIGURE 4.2.
MacPPP 2.2 running on a Powerbook Duo via a Global Village PowerPort Mercury modem.

Apple has also developed GeoPort technology. This is an innovative approach to modem communications that can allow DMA-serial port Macs to use part of the system's CPU to emulate a modem in software. The GeoPort Telecommunications Adapter is a small pod that connects to these Macs' serial ports in the standard modem fashion, and uses special GeoPort software to complete the package. The system can now emulate a 14.4K modem without any other connections. The main caveat to this approach is the load that the emulator can place on your CPU; the non-PowerPC AV Macs that can use GeoPort technology can experience a large percentage of CPU power being drained off to run the emulator. It's best to consider using the GeoPort adapter with a fast PowerMac only.

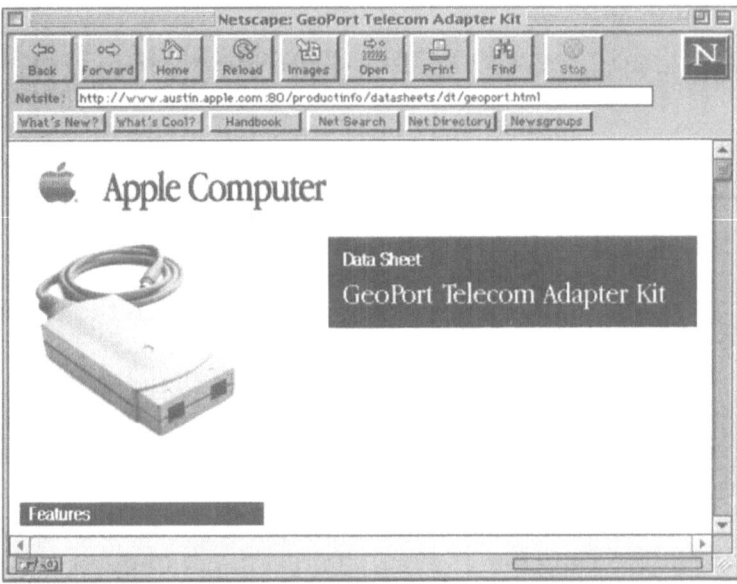

FIGURE 4.3.
GeoPort documents at Apple's Technical information Web site (www.info.apple.com).

Also, the cost differential between a low profile Mac modem like the Supra mentioned above (which won't eat into your CPU processor power) and the GeoPort Telecommunications Adapter may make fiddling with the GeoPort less appealing. GeoPort technology shows that Apple is leading with technological innovation; it may take the wide availability of much faster CPUs like the PPC604 to make it more feasible. Expect Apple to deliver an ISDN version of the GeoPort Telecom Adapter Kit around the time 604s are more prevalent in their desktop line. This would give GeoPort a definite edge over standard modems.

There are also a number of interesting ISDN modems and internal adapter cards available for the Macintosh. ISDN is rapidly becoming one of the best ways to connect to the Internet, and the speed at which it can run Netscape is the main reason why.

Analog vs. ISDN

Although the standard phone line system is all you really need to run Netscape, you'll find that it has built-in limitations that will affect the kind of performance you'll get. The standard POTS (Plain Old Telephone System) is still derived from analog technology, and geared for voice transmission. This means that the computer's digital information has to be converted to analog in order to transfer down the POTS line. That's what a standard modem does: it modulates digital computer signals into analog to send them out and demodulates them back into digital as they come in. An analog signal can be considered as an erratic wave formation. The information it transmits is passing over older circuits that were designed in the 1940s for voice, and the translated data has to make the analog journey back and forth in this inefficient format, not to mention the overhead involved in the translation process.

ISDN (Integrated Services Digital Network), on the other hand, uses a digital format from end to end. This means you don't need a modem; ISDN uses what's called a DSU (Data Service Unit) to move digital computer data over digital lines from end to end. This is more like a square wave, with no erratic acoustic patterning found in an analog signal. With more precise digital control over the data involved, a sustained high-speed connection can be made.

ISDN is becoming more and more available in residential versions and requires little extra equipment. Examples of ISDN equipment that will work with Macintosh at this time include the SAT-SAGEM Planet II ISDN card (internal NUBUS), the 3Com Impact and Motorola BitSURFR (external serial units), and the Motorola HMTA 200 hybrid modem (a combination external ISDN adapter and V32. modem).

SAT-SAGEM, a French company, has developed a series of internal ISDN cards for Macintosh. The Planet series uses an open slot on any NuBus-equipped Mac. Planet I is ISDN data-capable; Planet II also includes telephony options (and is a bit shorter than the 8-inch Planet I card, at 7 inches). These allow you to make synchronous (digital) connections to your access provider.

The only other equipment you'll need with this board is an NT1 adapter. This is a Network Termination unit; it connects your ISDN equipment to the ISDN equipment at your Internet access provider's site. It sits between your Mac's ISDN equipment and your ISDN phone jack. The Northern Telecom NT 1 Meridian,

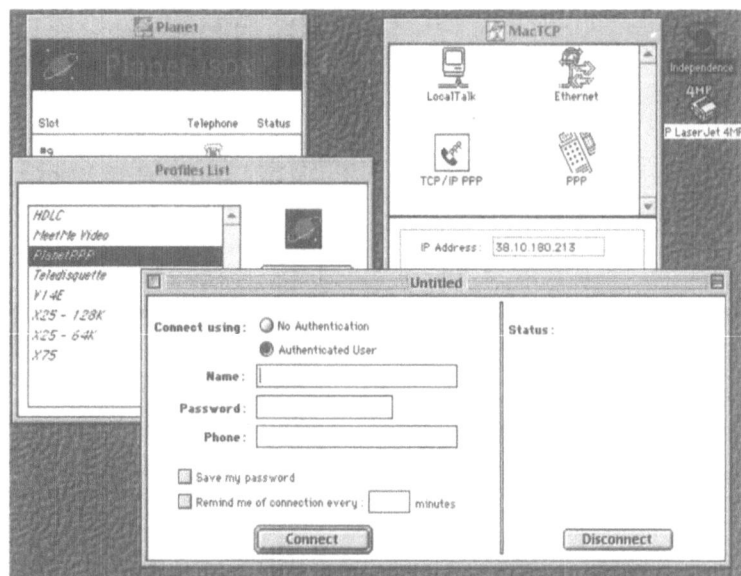

FIGURE 4.4.
SAT-SAGEM's Planet
ISDN software.

roughly the size of a standard external modem and desk- or wall-mountable, is offered by Bell Atlantic at $147, and SAT-SAGEM provides software drives for it, as well as for Bell Atlantic US-5ESS termination units. It's becoming more common for ISDN adapters to include Network Termination built into the base unit, and we expect the Planet series to support capability in the near future. The only serious fault with the Planet cards is in their relatively high cost; at $995 (plus the cost for the NT1 adapter, another $150), approximately four to five times the cost of a fast modem.

However, you do get a full Mac setup with true digital connectivity with the Planet series. SAT-SAGEM provides software for MacTCP, including a separate TCP/IP PPP extension you can configure in the same way as for PPP, as well as a connection utility that can also periodically remind you of the connection. The Planet II series also comes with a good set of documentation, including manuals for configuring PPP with an access provider like PSI.

Once you have the hardware installed and the access provider selected (make sure they are ISDN-capable), you have to have your ISDN line installed. Contact your local phone service to find out if ISDN is available in your area. Use the ISDN profiles provided by your Internet access provider to tell your phone company how to set up your line. In this case we used the profiles provided by PSI to order our ISDN line. The line can be installed either to a new phone jack or in the place of an existing line.

Costs for our example line (San Francisco area, Pacific Bell) ran to $75 for the installation labor, $35 to switch the line from a standard analog line to a digital line, and $15 for the first monthly fee. For $125, we had a digital ISDN line that more closely approximated the high-speed networks that Mosaic was designed to be used with. A caveat to remember is that an ISDN line is not a standard phone line; if you change an old line over, you can't use standard modems, phones, or FAX equipment with it any longer (you can even possibly damage a standard phone by connecting it to an ISDN jack). Special ISDN telecommunications equipment is available, but it's certainly not as common as analog equipment.

Once you have the ISDN line in, you can use the Planet software to configure your Internet access software for MacTCP and Planet's TCP/IP PPP extension, which you will use in the place of MacPPP. Follow the instructions for entering in your Domain Name Server exactly as you would with standard PPP. Then use the PlanetPPP software to create a new connection profile, and enter your ISDN information, including your ISDN SPID (Service Profile ID) numbers provided by the phone company. You also set up your direct dial number to your access provider, and your account information (user name and password) if you need to use authentication.

You're now ready to set up a synchronous PPP link to the Internet. Start your connection by using the PlanetPPP application (use the connect and disconnect buttons to bring the link up and down), and you'll be connected to your service provider in ten seconds or less, without the standard modem connection screeches. You can begin to see the benefits immediately: as you start Netscape, the flow of data will be much faster and home pages will load at a smooth, rapid rate. You can now attempt to access larger multimedia sound, picture, and movie files with more reasonable downloading times.

Another type of ISDN adapter is one that connects to a serial port, like a modem. This would need an open serial port, and you should make sure AppleTalk is turned off if you use the printer port. PSI certifies the Motorola BitSURFR as a personal ISDN adapter. It includes an NT1 adapter, so you don't have to pay for additional hardware. It only runs on ISDN lines, and is somewhat limited in its connectivity to asynchronous PPP (analog modem-style). While faster data communications are achieved with this unit over standard modems, it uses the same type of data link as a standard modem, so it's not as fast as the synchronous PPP available with the Planet cards. Its primary advantages are its relatively low cost and the fact that you can move it between different systems and sites easily (for example, between Mac desktops and PowerBooks, and between home and office ISDN accounts). External ISDN units are generally easier to set up and configure with standard MacTCP and MacPPP software, almost like a modem. You should also note that Motorola doesn't include Macintosh software you can use to configure the BitSURFR, although they do give you instructions for programming it with a terminal program like ZTerm (in the event you have to change the default settings).

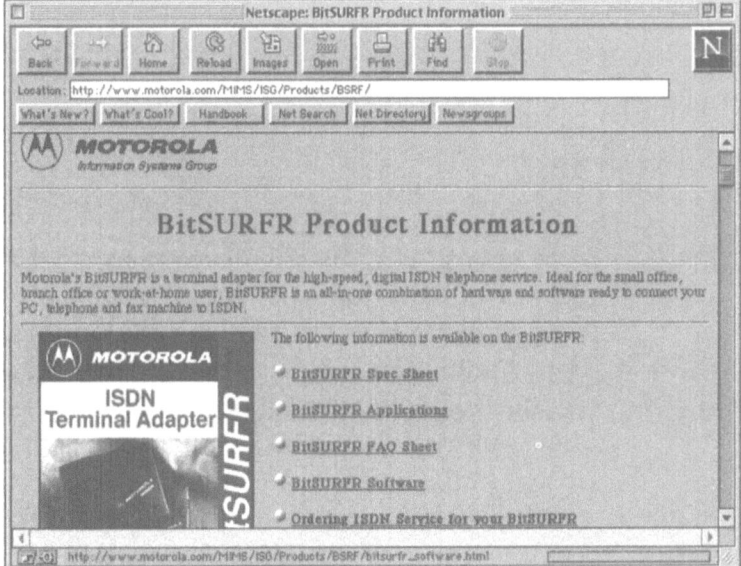

FIGURE 4.5.
The BitSURFR home page at Motorola's Web site.

You might want to consider an external ISDN unit that includes a modem, like Motorola's HMTA 200. This unit combines an ISDN terminal adapter with an integrated NT1 unit and a fast V32 14.4/28.8K modem. It not only works as an ISDN adapter (using your Mac's serial port, and subject to the same current limitations to asynchronous PPP as other external ISDN adapters), it also functions as an analog modem over your ISDN line. That means that you can connect to your Internet account via ISDN, and to an on-line service via the modem function. The HMTA 200 also fails to include Mac configuration software, so you'll have to program the unit from the front control panel via a small LCD display, or by commands via a terminal program like Zterm.

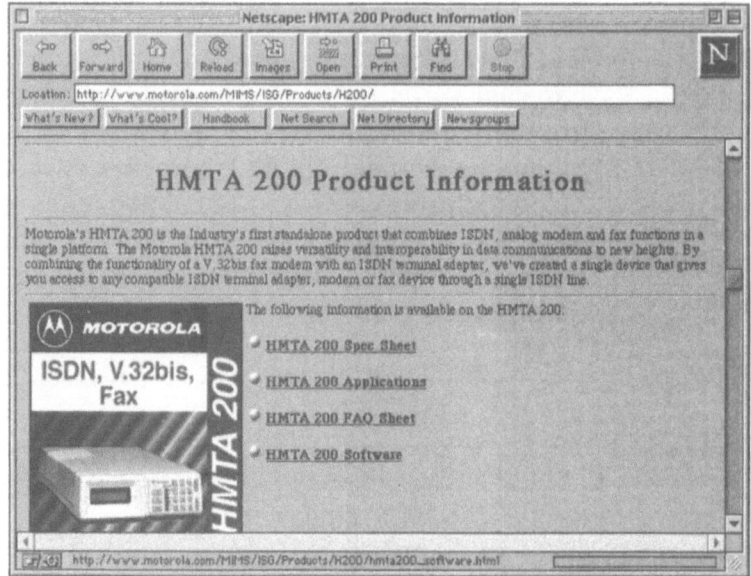

FIGURE 4.6.
Motorola's HMTA
200 (from the Web
site).

Note: You may be able to configure these units via the Windows configuration software Motorola provides, if you're running SoftWindows. Just launch the Configuration Manager under Windows and use it to download your settings for the units via the pseudo PC's serial port (COM1 or COM2). Exit Windows, and your Mac should be able to use the new settings for the unit stored in the unit's own memory.

3Com also has a hybrid modem and ISDN adapter, called the Impact (formerly the QuickAccess Remote). This works in the same manner as the HMTA 200, and also includes high-speed modem emulation. 3Com has provided software for the Macintosh for this unit (you can download it from ftp.3com.com in the /pub/adapters/macintosh directory). You can use this software to upgrade the unit's firmware and software configurations, and there are also instructions on how to connect your Mac via PPP with the Impact.

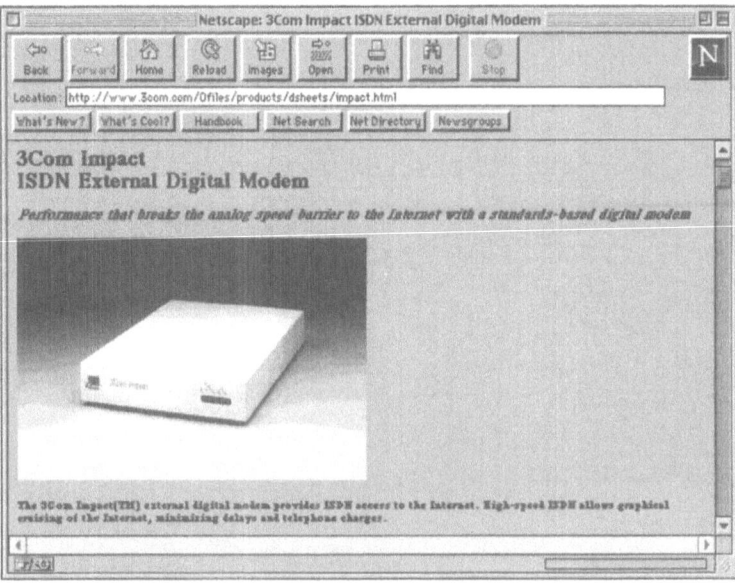

FIGURE 4.7.
The 3Com Impact page at the 3Com Web site.

The hybrid modem is a good solution to the problem of canceling an existing analog line by making it into a digital ISDN line. This unit gives you back the modem functionality thereby lost. Unfortunately, its asynchronous PPP ISDN connection is still not the same as a full-on synchronous PPP link, which you can only get with an internal card like the Planet series.

It's especially interesting to note how the ISDN service provider, your Internet access provider, the ISDN hardware, and your Internet software all interrelate. In this case, the ISDN service provider brought the line to the Macintosh, configuring the line to match the ISDN adapter card or external unit. The ISDN equipment was certified by PSI as compatible with their Internet service, and was listed as being compatible with Macintosh Internet connectivity software. This meant that MacTCP and MacPPP were already verified as working with PSI via this equipment, so configuration was easy. It's important to have this same chain working for whatever Macintosh ISDN Internet equipment you choose.

5
Venturing onto the Net

Netscape: The Home Page

The Netscape Communications home page is a great place to
start your tour of the Internet and the World Wide Web. While
the contents will certainly change over time, you can expect to
see some similar elements like the ones that follow.

The main Web site for Netscape loads automatically when you
start the program. Here you can read about Netscape news and
planned upgrades. You can also reach a wide range of services
from the large image map at the top of the page, or from the
subject links below. (See Figure 5.1.)

The first section on the left leads to the Exploring the Net
area. This corresponds to the directory buttons on the Netscape
browser itself, and has information on cool sites, places to find
new Web pages, direct links to subjects in the Yahoo Web directory, and the best selection of Internet search tools available. (See
Figure 5.2.)

The next section gives you information on Netscape itself, the
company and its products. You can also find out about Netscape
sales programs, development partnerships, and business oppor-
tunities. (See Figure 5.3.)

You can also try out electronic commerce at the Netscape Gen-

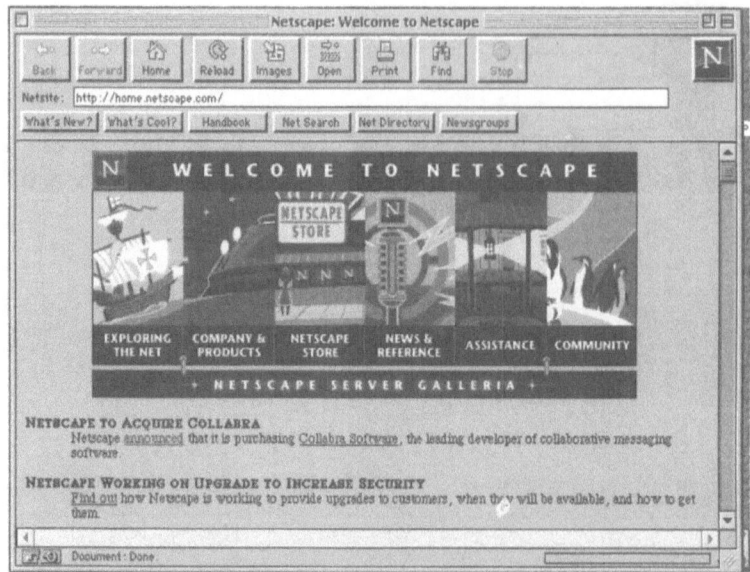

FIGURE 5.1.
Netscape
Communications'
Home Page.

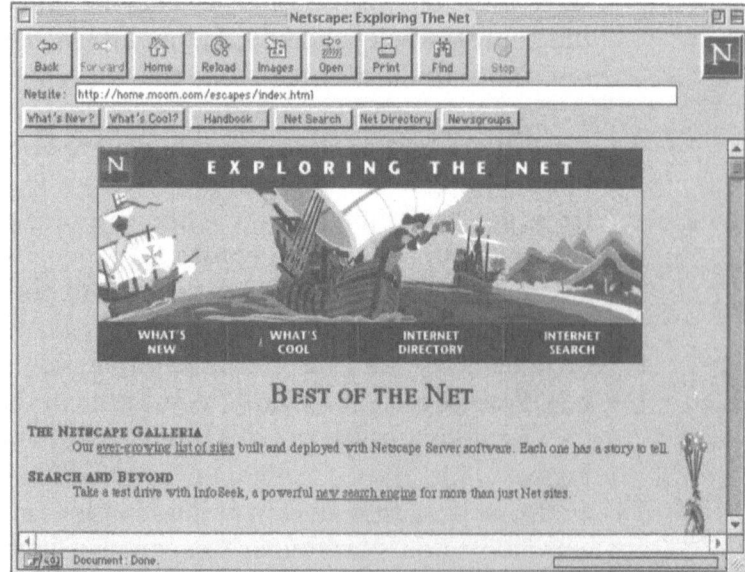

FIGURE 5.2.
The Exploring the
Net section of the
Netscape home
page.

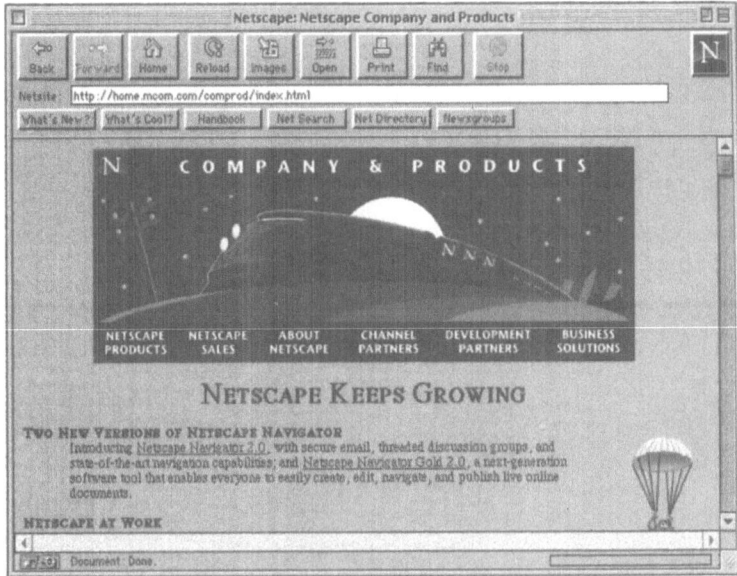

FIGURE 5.3.
The Company & Products section of the Netscape home page.

eral Store. Shop for software, publications, and support contracts right from your Netscape browser. There's also a bazaar of companies offering products over the Web. (See Figure 5.4.)

Check the News & Reference section for news updates, including daily headlines and Netscape press releases. There are also links to standards documentation (find out more about what new Internet proposals are really all about) and on-line reference materials. (See Figure 5.5.)

Go directly to the Assistance section to find out how to set up your Netscape Web browser to its fullest capability. There are areas that can get you to on-line technical support and provide you with links to the best helper applications. You can also find out about training programs, and information on how to create your own Web sites. Check out the About the Internet section to find out more about the Web itself. (See Figure 5.6.)

Netscape has a number of User Groups located around the world, and you can find out about them at the Community section. There's also a link here to the Internet White Pages, where you can look up people on-line. (See Figure 5.7.)

Finally, check out the Netscape Galleria page to find an index of the most innovative Web sites that are using Netscape's advanced server technology. There are some very interesting sites listed here, with the best in Web craftsmanship. (See Figure 5.8.)

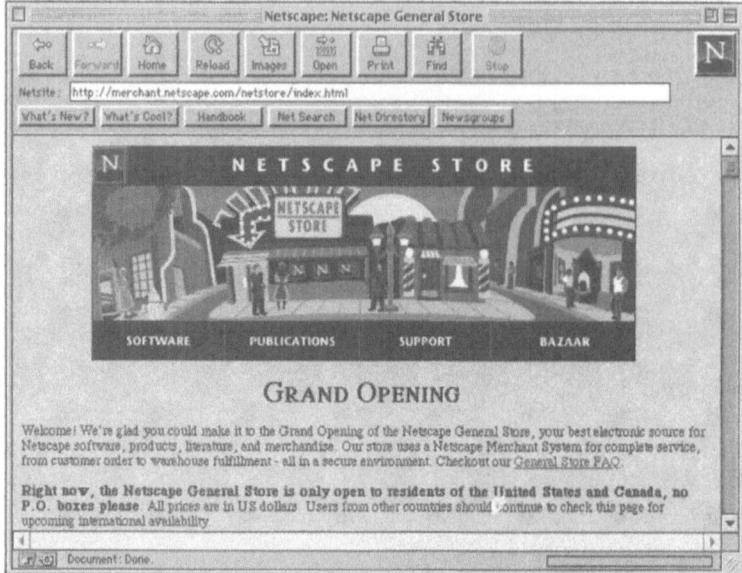

FIGURE 5.4.
The Netscape
Company Store.

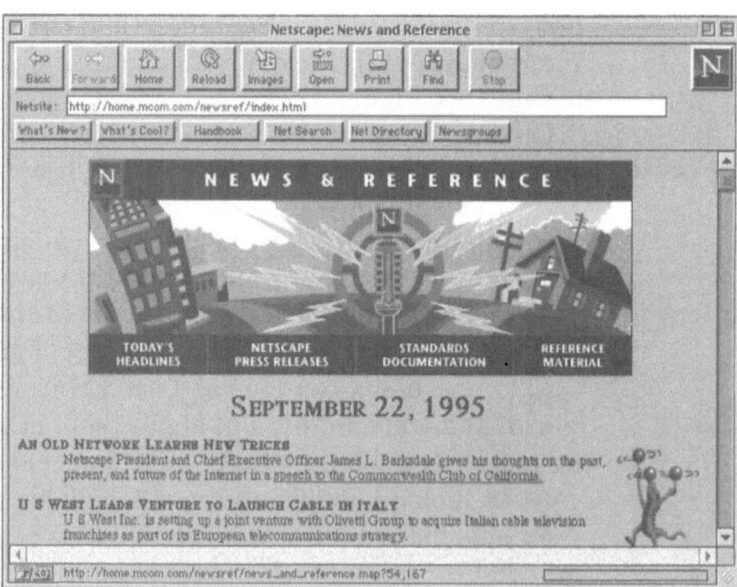

FIGURE 5.5.
The News &
Reference section at
the Netscape home
page.

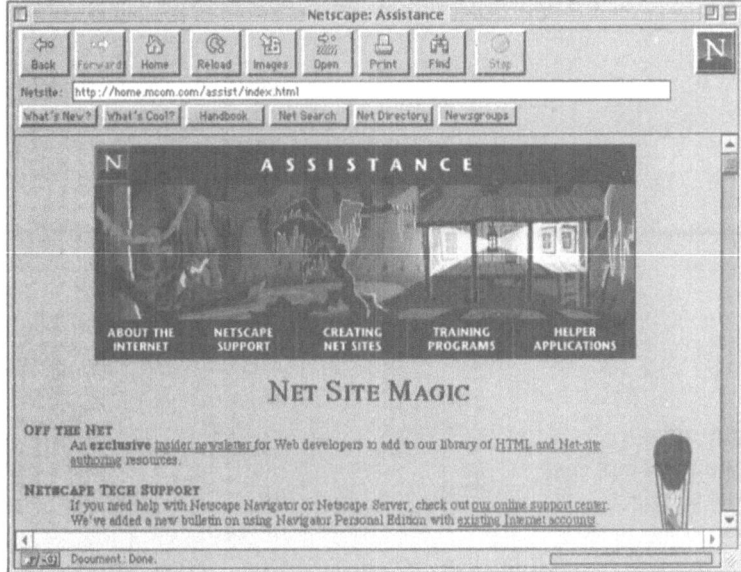

FIGURE 5.6.
The Assistance section at the Netscape home page.

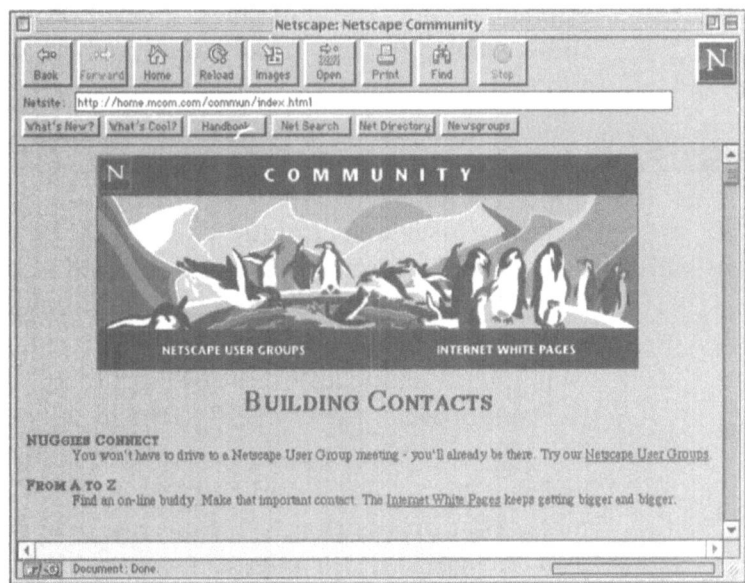

FIGURE 5.7.
The Community section at the Netscape home page.

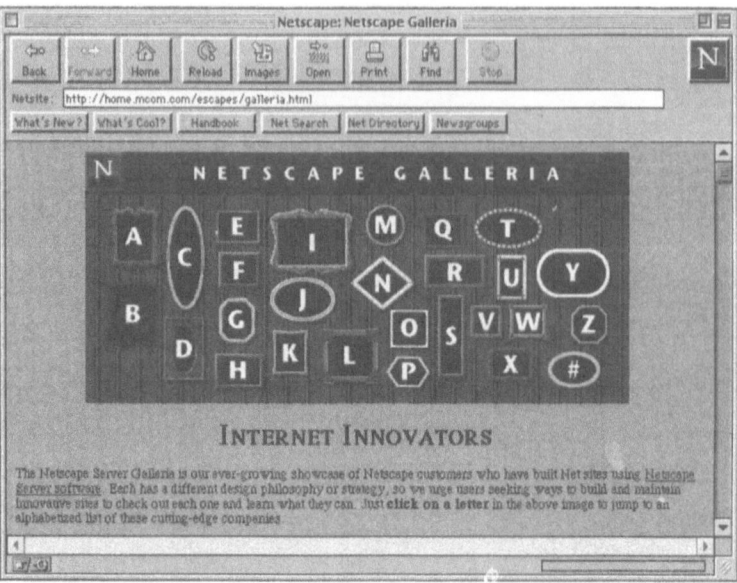

FIGURE 5.8.
The Netscape
Galleria page.

Once you've thoroughly investigated the Netscape Web site, you can go directly to the great area that is the World Wide Web. You'll need to know about the different types of Web sites that Netscape can access in order to make your Web browsing more profitable. These sites include Web pages, FTP directories, and gopher servers. You don't need special programs to reach any of these; Netscape can connect to all of them using URL protocols.

URL Protocols

Netscape uses a technique called TCP/IP to transfer information over the Internet. This information comes in a variety of formats, including text, pictures, compressed binary computer programs, and sound files. It's stored in many different ways as well, including file archives (FTP protocol), gopher indexes, and the Web browser format HTTP (the hypertext transfer protocol). The URL (Uniform Request Locator) was designed to allow Web browsers to act as central clearinghouses for these different formats. That means that Netscape can read hypertext documents in its own HTML format, access gopher indexes and FTP sites, and even read Network Newsgroups all within its main program window.

The first URL protocol type you'll come across is HTTP. Your default home page is in this format. This protocol allows the transfer of documents with links to remote Internet sites and picture and sound file links embedded in them. When you click on a highlighted picture icon, the HTTP protocol negotiates between your computer and the remote server computer, requests the picture, and downloads it to your local system. HTTP also handles links to other Internet sites via hot-linked words or pictures. HTTP's main format is HTML, the hypertext markup language. HTML is a file type; it's designed to give Netscape and other Web browsers the foundations to build a hypertext document out of text and picture files found on the Internet (or even on your local system, as in the Spyglass Enhanced NSCA Mosaic help system).

A sample of this can be viewed in Netscape. Launch the application, and you should see the Netscape default home page. Next, select the Source item under the View menu.

FIGURE 5.9.
Netscape and HTML
source code.

Note how the page is constructed of the body text with marked pointers to hypertext information and Internet sites. Netscape directly translates these tags into the related links and images and loads the page in the more-familiar Web document format, using the HTTP protocol.

Other URL types include FTP, gopher, and NNTP (Network News Transfer Protocol). Netscape can also load some file types directly; for example, you can load .TXT files directly into any Netscape Web browser version's main window. Some Web browsers for Macintosh also have a drag-and-drop feature that allows you to drag a file (HTML, text, or graphics) into their main windows, where it will load automatically. Netscape also loads .JPG and .GIF files directly into its main window, while other browsers may have to launch an external viewer for these types of files (although at least .GIF is supported by all browsers, some still lack in-line JPEG support). InterCon's Netshark browser can also load PICT files in-line.

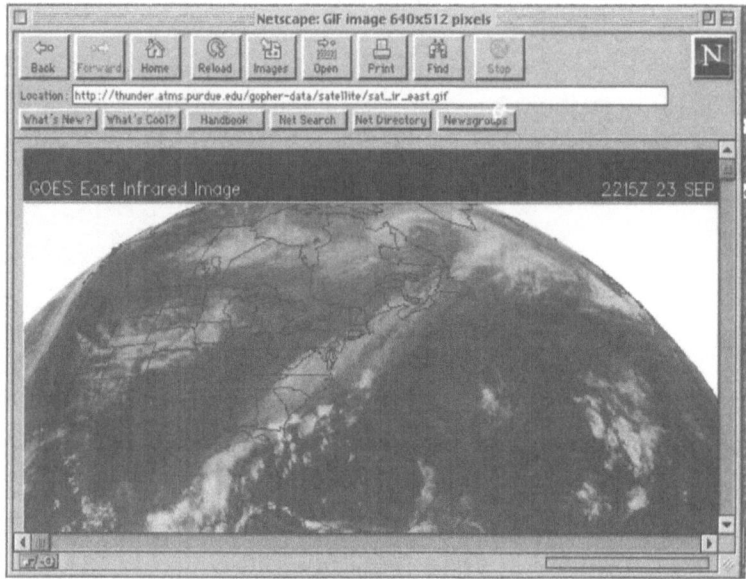

FIGURE 5.10.
Netscape's in-line image capabilities, showing an up-to-the-minute weather image GIF file.

Most of the URL types that Netscape can access directly are preconfigured. This means that they'll work with your version without any more work on your part. A link on the Netscape home page to the FTP site where the files are located will bring up an FTP archive automatically, for example. One exception is NetNews; Netscape can only access the worldwide network discussion groups and NetNews file archives directly if you have a valid News server. This is a part of a good Internet access provider account, so make sure your access provider gives you the name of a News server that you can configure properly. Netscape is still the best Web browser you can use to run NetNews.

To configure NetNews to work with your copy of Netscape, make sure your Internet access provider has given you the name of your default News server. Like the DNS (Domain Name Server) system that resolves Internet addresses for Netscape, the News server collects Net Newsgroup postings from the Internet and transmits them to your system. It's another computer your Mac will connect to in the background to receive News.

In our example, our access provider PSI has provided us with a News server address as part of our password-protected Internet access account. Accessing our carefully preserved documentation, we see that our NNTP News server at PSI is called usenet.interramp.com. We can now open up Netscape's Preferences panel (under the Options menu), and put this line into the News server field. You can also set the maximum number of articles to show in a News session here; reducing the number from the default setting of 100 may be helpful if you have a slow connection. With your PPP connection up, use the Newsgroups directory button (or the Directory menu item) to go to NetNews. The resultant newsgroup interface looks like this:

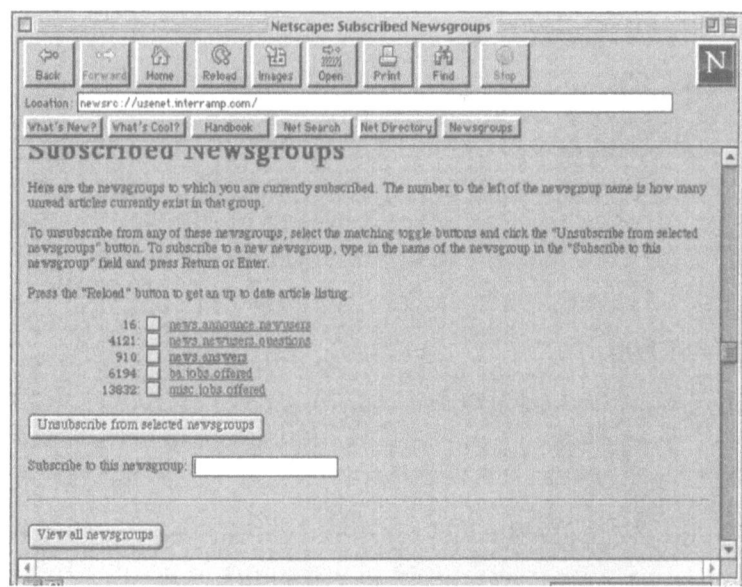

FIGURE 5.11.
Netscape's NetNews interface with PSI's Newsfeed, showing subscribed newsgroups.

This is your newsrc (news resource) file, showing your subscribed newsgroups. The default newsgroups you will be subscribed to are those for new users, like news.announce.newusers, news.newusers.questions, and news.answers. You can unsubscribe from these new user groups (after you've investigated them —they're still the best places to get familiar with reading and posting NetNews articles) by placing a check mark in the box to the left side of the name, and hitting the Unsubscribe button. You can also do this with any other newsgroups you may subscribe to in the future.

To subscribe to newsgroups, you can build your newsrc by selecting newsgroup names from a list. Click on the "View All Newsgroups" button to download an interactive list of all newsgroups currently available from your News server. Here's where you may be able to tell if your Internet access provider is "pre-screening" your News feed; some of the more controversial newsgroups may be completely missing from this list. You can consider asking your access provider if they have a full, unrestricted news feed before you sign up.

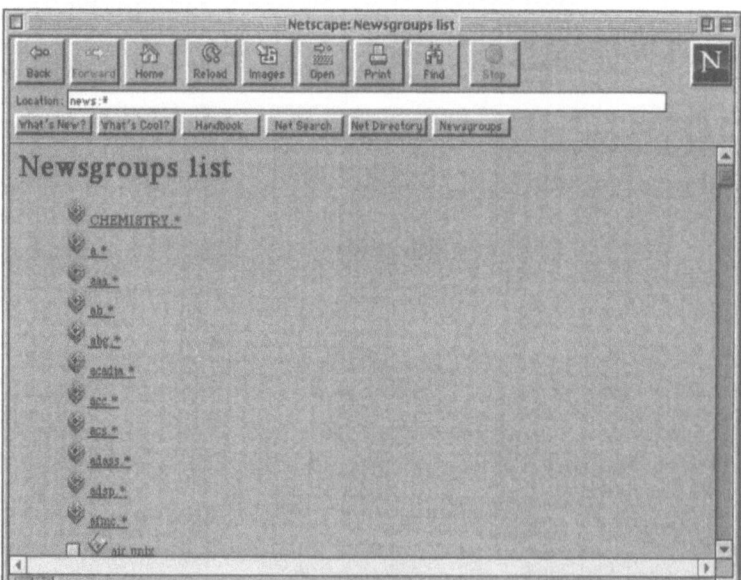

FIGURE 5.12.
"View All Newsgroups" list showing a full News feed.

In the Newsgroups list, the yellow news bundles indicate that there are more newsgroups in a submenu under the particular topic. Click on the link to move further down the topic list. A single newspaper icon indicates you've reached a particular newsgroup. You can subscribe to this group by placing a check mark in the box to the left of it. It will then go into your `newsrc`, and show up in your list of "Subscribed Newsgroups" the next time you hit the Newsgroups directory button.

You can go to newsgroups directly from the "Subscribed Newsgroups" screen. Just click on the name of the newsgroup (the number of articles available is noted to the left of the name, and this will let you judge how long you may have to wait to receive them). You'll get a list of readable articles and message threads, along with icons that will help you to navigate the newsgroup.

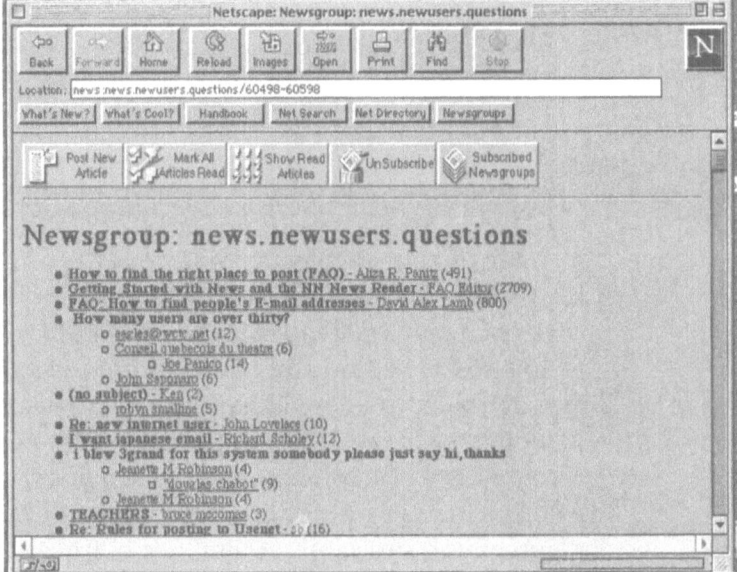

FIGURE 5.13. Netscape's News interface, showing the `news.announce. newusers` newsgroup.

Use the Post New Article button to submit a new article to the newsgroup you're currently reading. This will activate Netscape's combined Send Mail/Post News panel, where you can easily compose an article and send it off. To add a signature file (a short description/disclaimer/information panel) to your news posts, use SimpleText or another word processor to make a short text file, then launch Netscape's Options/Preferences panel, and go to the Mail and News section. Under the Mail section, click on the File setting, and use the Browse button to locate your signature file. This should append your signature file to your news posts, and let you attach contact information easily without having to retype it for each message.

You can also quote the text from a document here (for example,

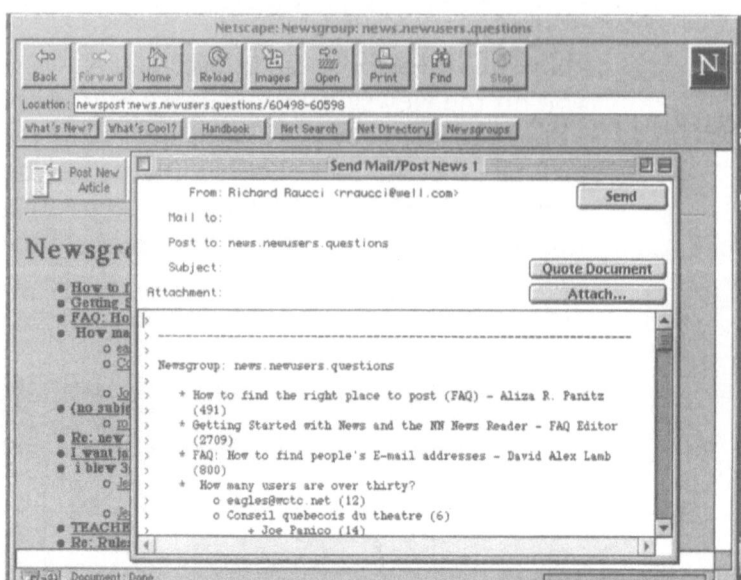

FIGURE 5.14.
Netscape's Post News panel.

to refer to a news posting in a follow-up message), or attach a file (in text format) to your posting.

Netscape's Newsreader interface also has buttons you can use to unsubscribe from the particular Newsgroup you've reached, and get back to your Subscribed list as well. To read the News, just click on a message subject line. The number to the right of the subject name refers to the size (in lines) of the news message. A sizable news posting can take a long time to transmit, especially if you have a slow connection. For our example, we've gone back to the Newsgroup view for the news.announce.newusers group, and clicked on the "How to find the right place to post" FAQ (Frequently Asked Questions) news message.

It's important to note that News postings move continually forward; messages are not saved for a long period of time, and the postings in a particular group will change over time. You may not find this particular news article in this group at the time you make your connection, for example. But the newusers groups usually repost these types of articles fairly frequently, so you should be able to find an article of interest at almost any time.

Once you've reached an actual posting, you'll see buttons for following the message thread (this allows you to move through a group of postings on the same subject), and for posting follow-up messages and replies. You can also get back to the main list

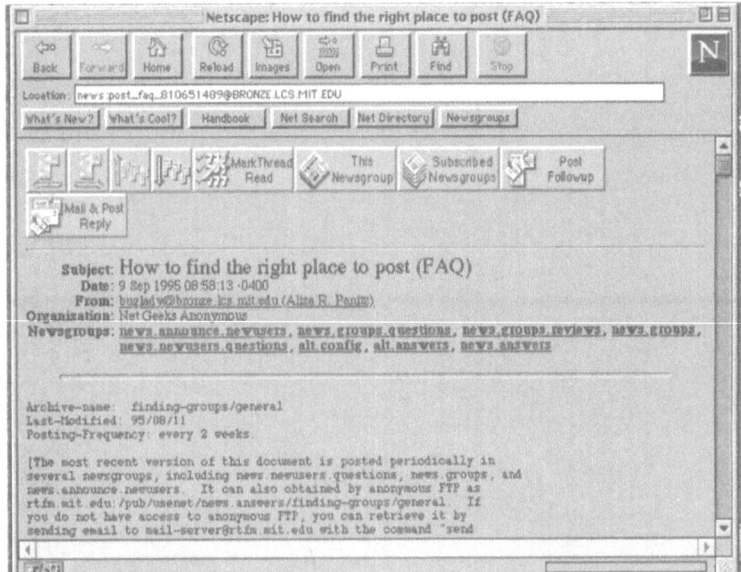

FIGURE 5.15.
The "How to find
the right place to
post" FAQ UseNet
news article from
the news.announce.
newusers
newsgroup.

of articles by clicking on the "This Newsgroup" button.

If you want to browse newsgroups in a free-form manner, you can use the "View All Newsgroups" button from the Subscribed Newsgroups screen to get a list of all the groups available from your news server, and access them directly from their hyper-linked names. You don't have to subscribe to a group first to read it. Also, you can look for a particular topic in all of the news-groups available by using the search panel located at the very end of the list. Since this search engine can look inside nested groups, it can be very useful for building your subscription list, or to just browse.

Look for a copy of Netscape 2.0 for an updated News reader interface that works mostly like the one described above, but includes some minor cosmetic improvements (including a reader panel that's separate from the main browser, that allows you to see the Newsgroup structure while you read messages).

6
Gophers, Web Encyclopedias, and Search Engines

Gopher is a way to search for information over the Internet. The gopher protocols were developed to help manage the sheer volume of information present. These allow for large amounts of text to be stored in servers that are as easily accessible to browsers as FTP file directories. Gopher servers can also contain picture and sound files. However, gophers are not technically HTML Web-based information sources (meaning they won't display as nicely as a standard hypertext home page). You'll have to go to a Web "encyclopedia" like Yahoo to find information in Web format. You can also find information on the World Wide Web by using a number of Internet search engines. These allow you to look up topics of interest, and then build a hypertext list of references you can go to with your browser.

We'll first look at the gopher server. A base-level gopher is still accessible from a terminal shell type of Internet account.

Gophers use search engine protocols like Veronica and Jughead. These are standard ways to access information using a variety of intelligent software query types.

What this means to the general Netscape user is that they can access information on gopher servers by looking it up. These interfaces are all available for use with the Web browsers that

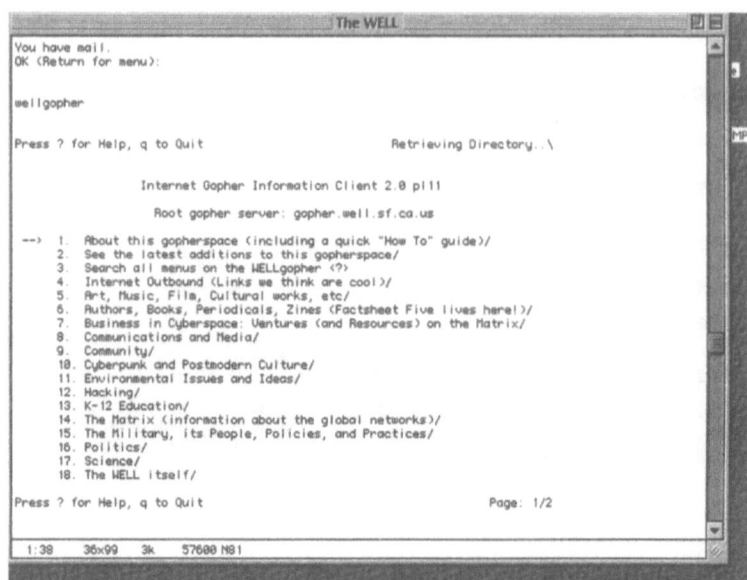

FIGURE 6.1.
The text-based
gopher at the WELL
in Sausalito.

we've covered in earlier chapters. Make sure your browser can
support forms; every version of Netscape has this capability.

Netscape can read a gopher file type directly. A look at the same
gopher server as displayed before, but now in a hypertext Web
format is seen in Figure 6.2.

The Internet Outbound link at the WELL leads to a link for
searching Gopherspace with Veronica. This will present you with
a list of Veronica search engines at various locations around the
world. You might also want to look at the Veronica FAQs and
on-line tutorials located here. (See Figure 6.3.)

Pick the Veronica search engine located closest to you to speed
up your search. We went to the one at PSINet, and entered the
term "pregnancy." The results are presented in a gopher format,
but are arranged from a wide range of sources. Place the mouse
pointer over a link to see where it's from and what type of data
it is. (See Figure 6.4.)

You can search this page directly by using the Find command
under the Edit menu. Click on the items with text icons to view
them directly in Netscape, and move to gophers across the Net by
clicking on directory folders. There may also be binary pictures
and sound files you can load and view here. (See Figure 6.5.)

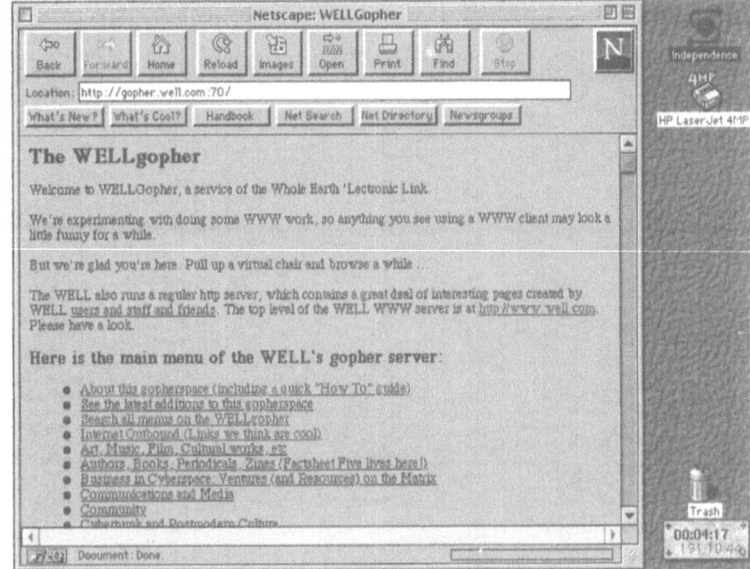

FIGURE 6.2.
The WELLgopher in Netscape.

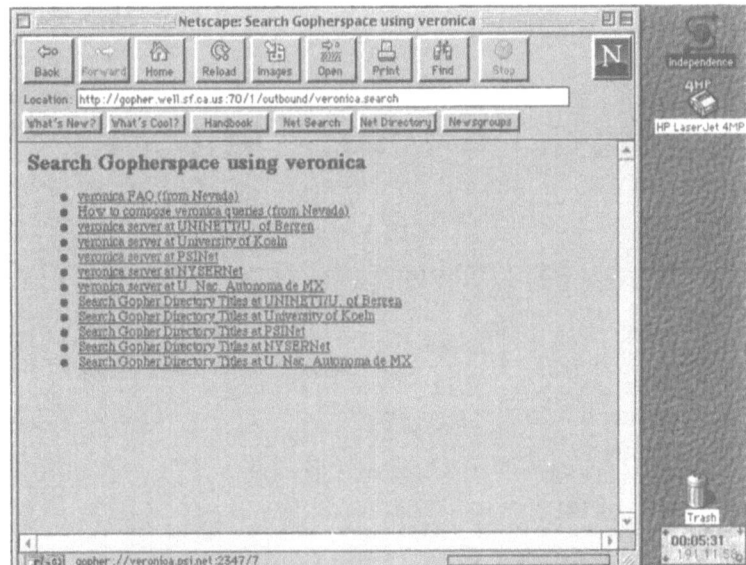

FIGURE 6.3.
The "Search Gopherspace using veronica" page at the WELLgopher.

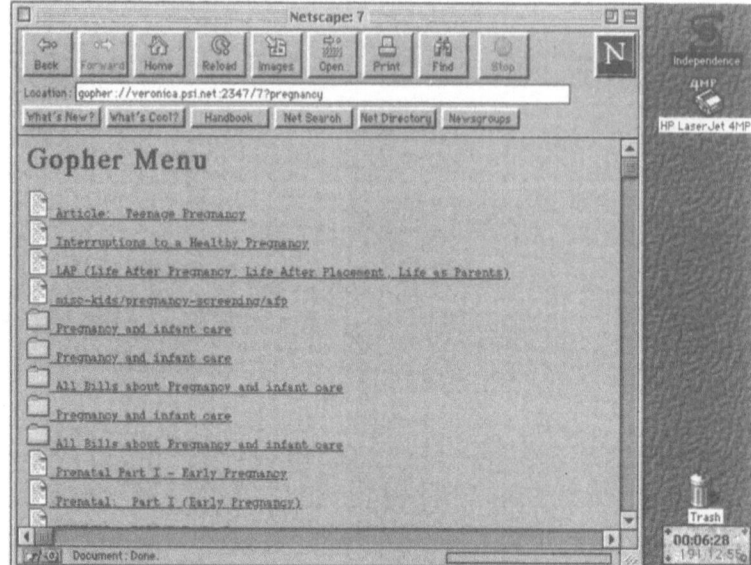

FIGURE 6.4.
The Gopher Menu
results from
PSINet's Veronica
search on the term
"pregnancy."

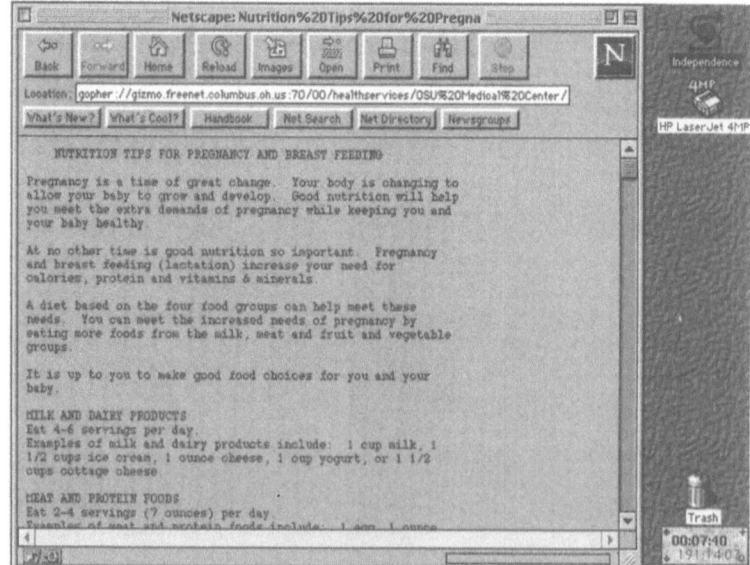

FIGURE 6.5.
A text document
from the Veronica
search results on the
term "pregnancy"
on PSINet's gopher
(Nutrition Tips for
Pregnancy and
Breast-feeding).

Gopherspace is a wide-ranging information source, and you can find a lot of useful information here. You may also want to try the USC Gopher Jewels site (gopher://cwis.usc.edu:70) as a good jumping-off point for gopher server browsing.

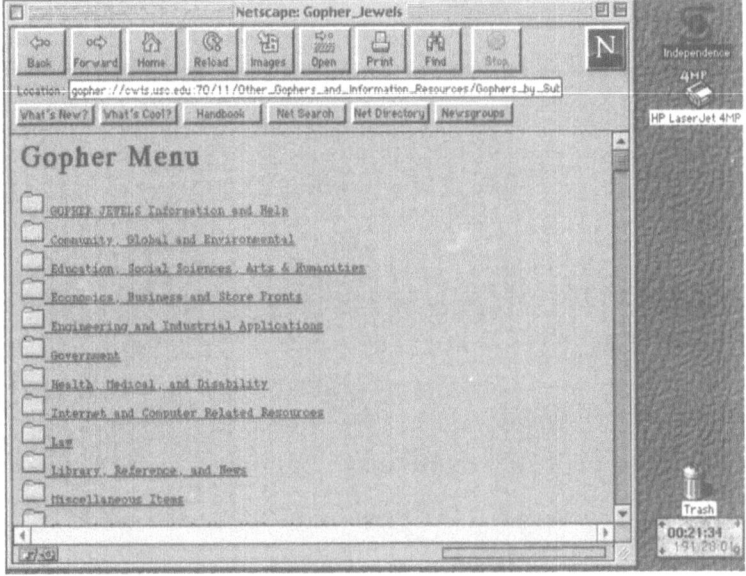

FIGURE 6.6.
The USC Gopher Jewels gopher site, in Web browser format.

By following the Community, Global, and Environmental link, you can find lists of gophers by country and state, as well as gopher information on environmental issues. You'll also be able to search the entire gopher server from each submenu. We've followed the links to "Other State Gophers," and are presented with a hypertext list of US State gopher servers, with annotations. (See Figure 6.7.)

You can search this list with the local Find panel, and go to the subjects by clicking on the links.

The University of Minnesota (UM) gopher provides a good look at how Gopher is changing to fit in more closely with the hyper-text format of the Web. Find it at gopher://gopher.micro.umn.edu. The UM site also has links to all of the gopher servers in the world, so you'll be able to spend a lot of time looking up information here. (See Figure 6.8.)

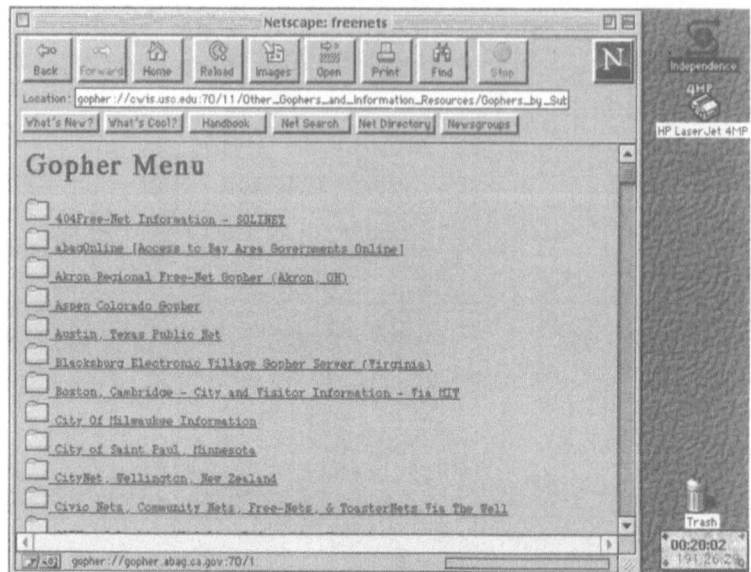

FIGURE 6.7.
The Gopher Jewels
state gopher server
listing.

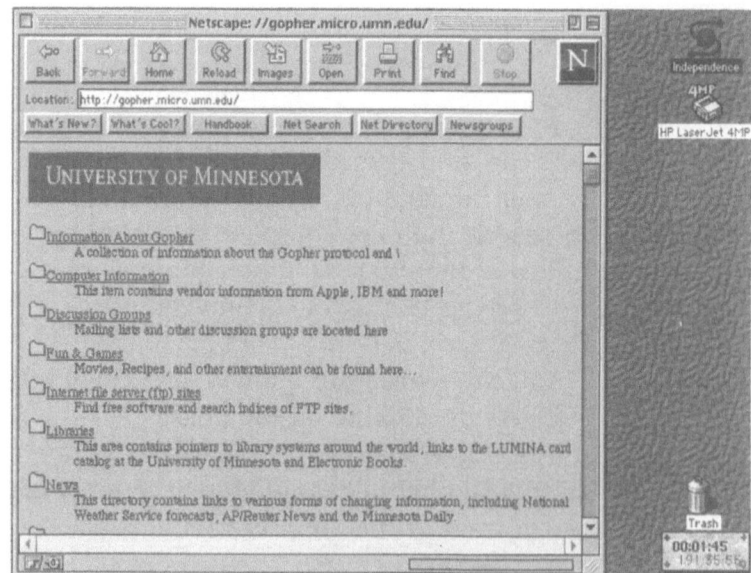

FIGURE 6.8.
The University of
Minnesota gopher
server in Web
hypertext format.

Web-Based Encyclopedias

You may also want to find Web pages with information resources that are in good old hypertext format, with in-line images, formatted text, and multimedia sound, and animation links.

The Yahoo Directory is a good place to find Web sites on various topics, and it also includes a search engine. You can reach it from Netscape by clicking on the Net Directory button, or directly from www.yahoo.com.

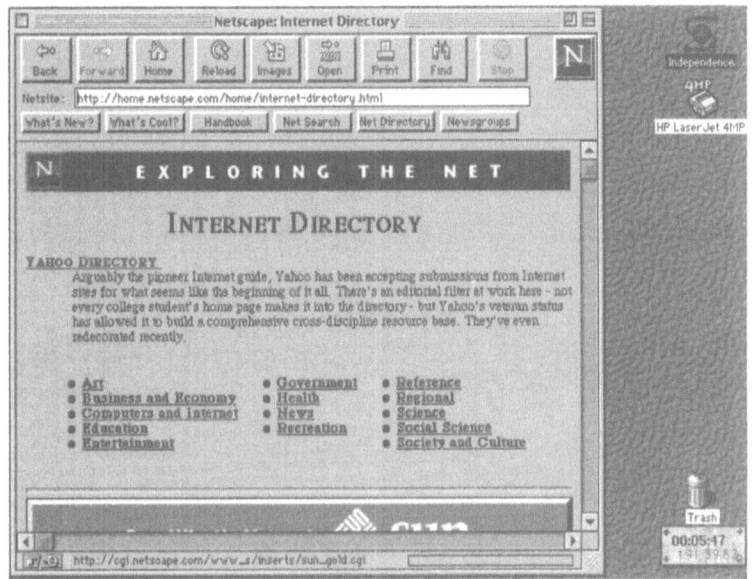

FIGURE 6.9.
Yahoo subject listings at Netscape's Internet Directory page.

Categories at Yahoo include the Arts, Business and Economy, Computers and the Internet, Education, Entertainment, Government, Health, News, Recreation, Reference, Regional, Society and Culture, and Science. Each category listing features a wide range of subjects, often leading to further subtopics. For example, the Health category leads to Web information on subjects like Alternative Medicine, Emergency Services, Environmental Health, Fitness, Health Care, Nutrition, Pharmacology, and Workplace health issues. (See Figure 6.10.)

You can explore the index directly by following a subject link down to another subject list. For example, the Nursing topic under Health leads to nursing-related newsgroups and information servers, Web sites and nursing school home pages, and a subsection on Midwifery. (See Figures 6.11 and 6.12.)

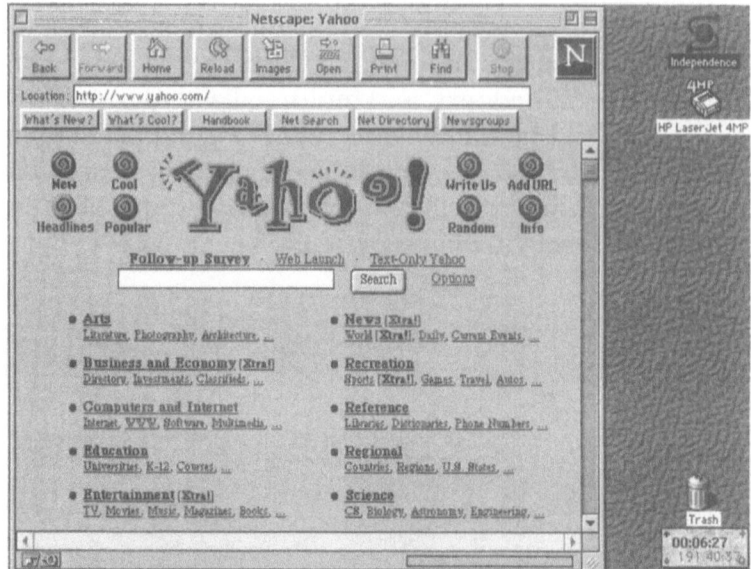

FIGURE 6.10.
The Yahoo Directory
home page.

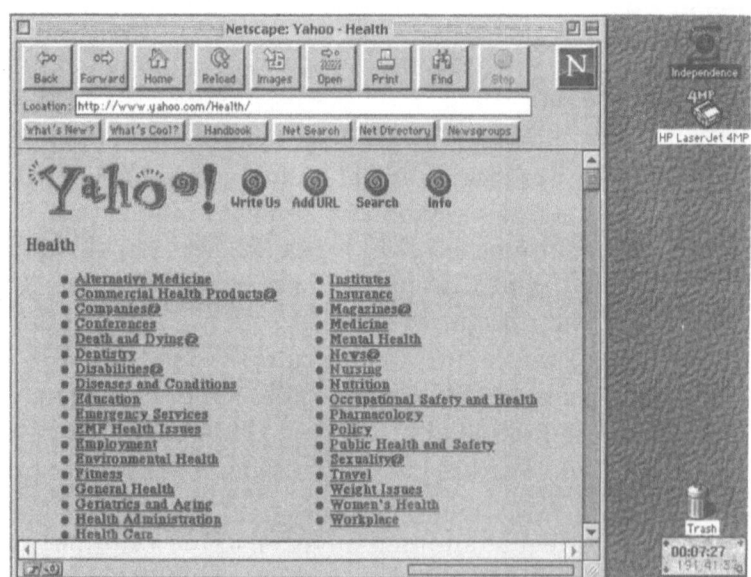

FIGURE 6.11.
The Yahoo Directory
Health topic index.

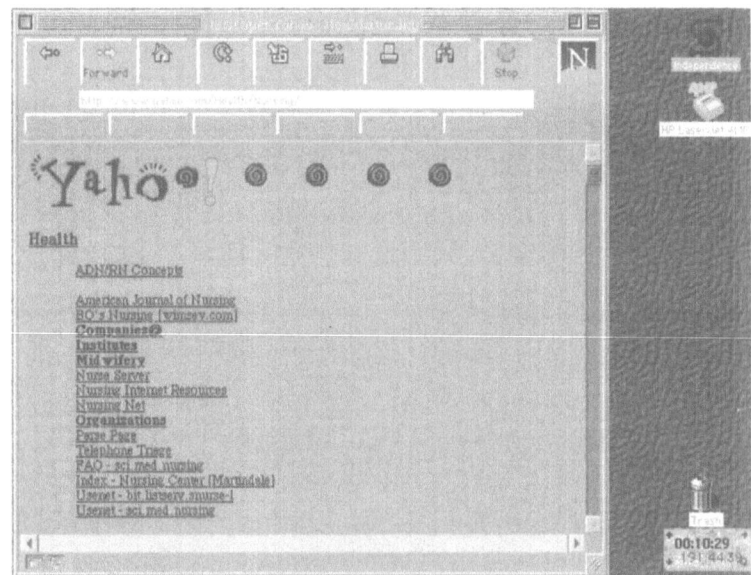

FIGURE 6.12.
The Yahoo Directory
Health/Nursing
index.

We can follow the Midwifery link to that subsection. Note that the index subjects in bold type lead to subsections; the number of listings in the subsection is listed to the right. (See Figure 6.13.)

We're now at the bottom level of this particular subject trail, and we can see a link that goes to a site listed for Midwifery, Pregnancy, and Birth-Related Information. This brings up a Web site off of Yahoo that provides a good index to information on this subject. (See Figure 6.14.)

You can look for information on any subject across the Web via Yahoo just by browsing. It's a good way to find interesting sites and related information. Use Netscape's Add Bookmarks function to keep a record of sites you've reached, so you don't have to remember your trail.

You can also search Yahoo directly. This will allow you to bypass the browsing method and get a hypertext list of Yahoo sections that relate to your topic. Just enter your search term in the panel at Yahoo's home page, and you'll be able to go directly to the information you want.

We entered our term "pregnancy," and the search results looked as seen in Figure 6.15.

This results list shows the places at Yahoo where the term is present. Notice that the information is not just in the Health section; there are also listings in the Arts, Society and Culture, and

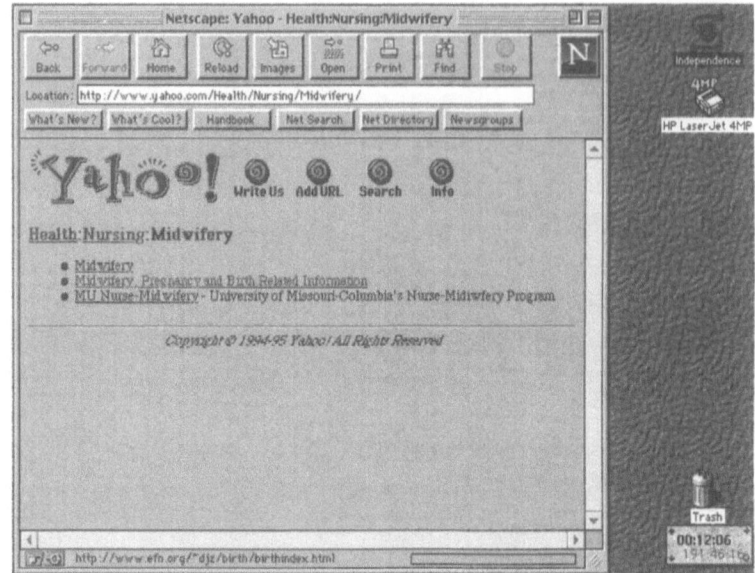

FIGURE 6.13.
The Yahoo Directory
Health/Nursing/
Midwifery index.

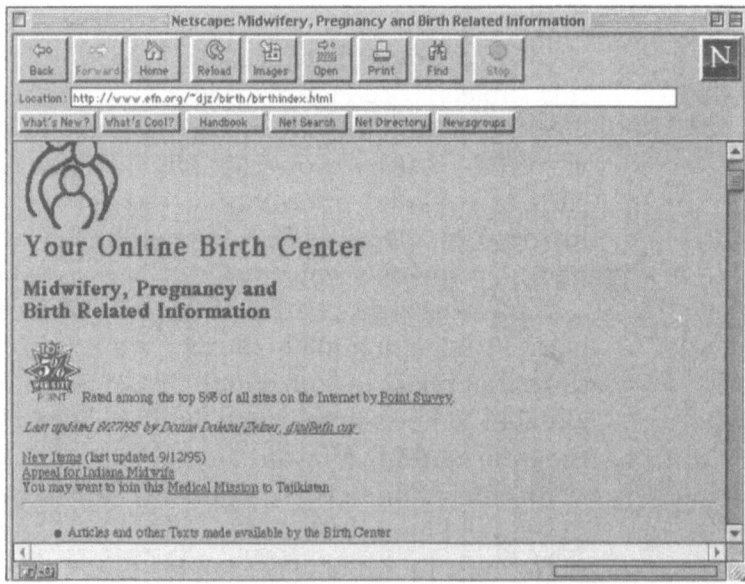

FIGURE 6.14.
The Online Birth
Center.

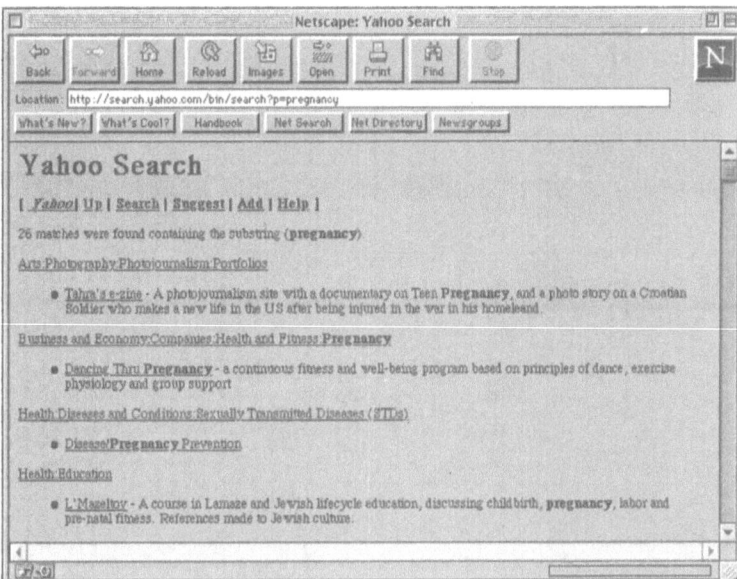

FIGURE 6.15.
Search results at
Yahoo for the term
"pregnancy."

Business sections, on topics including education, family planning, and pregnancy services. You have to go to the sites themselves to see if the information has value for you, and you can do that right from this list directly, just by clicking on a link.

For example, the FamilyWeb site under Society and Culture: Birth looks interesting. We can go to that home page, and access the relative link for their section on pregnancy for more information. (See Figure 6.16.)

You can search for information on any topic at Yahoo in this manner. The information base is growing rapidly, and chances are that there is a Web site with the information that you're looking for indexed here.

Advanced Web Searches

Netscape provides an easy link to several advanced search types from its Net Search page. You can access this from the button bar just by clicking on Net Search. Note that these search engines differ from Yahoo's in that they search a collection of Web page references from across the Internet, and are (for the most part) not as well edited. (See Figure 6.17.)

This brings up a well-indexed page of search tools, with helpful

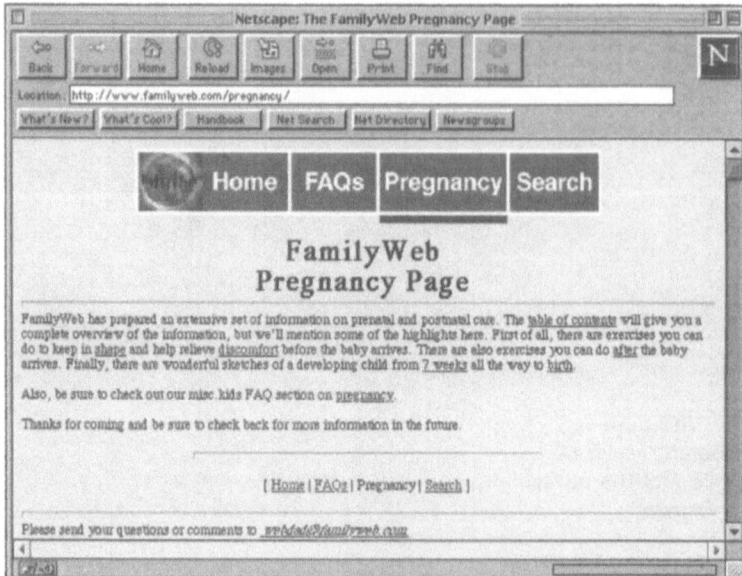

FIGURE 6.16.
The FamilyWeb
Pregnancy page.

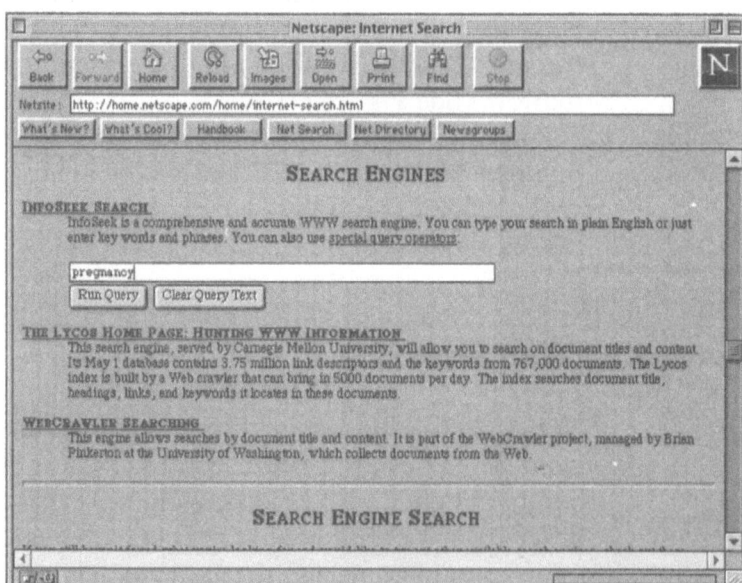

FIGURE 6.17.
Search engines at
Netscape's Net
Search page.

examples and descriptions. Some of these include Web crawlers, specialized search engines that can find information on the Internet via descriptive indices that the programs construct themselves.

The InfoSeek search panel is presented directly at Netscape's Net Search page, as Yahoo does with their home page. Just enter your term in here, and hit the Run Query button. You'll get a list of search results on your topic with brief descriptions and direct links. InfoSeek also provides on-line help for improving your Internet searches.

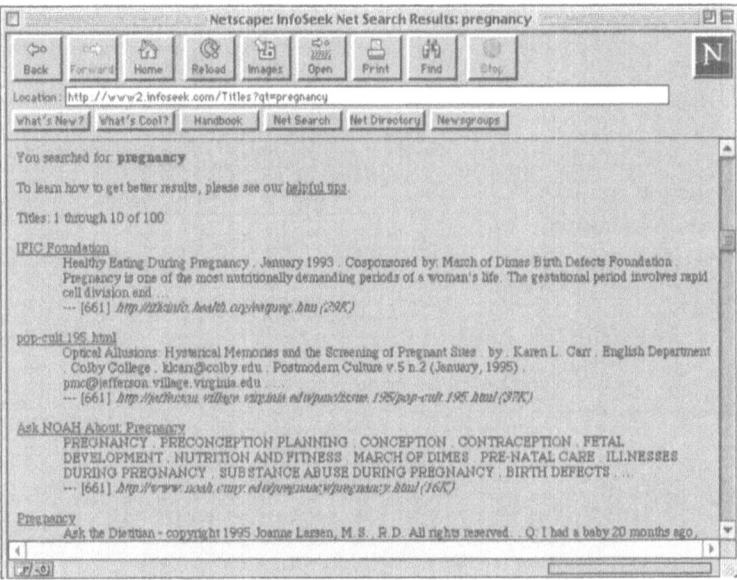

FIGURE 6.18.
InfoSeek results for the term "pregnancy."

You can also use the Lycos Web crawler at Carnegie-Mellon University in the same manner. It maintains a list of over 3 million Internet references, and it's growing. It uses software robots to gather information for its database by actively looking out over the Internet for new references. You can also set the search parameters in a number of different ways, including limiting the number of responses and the extent of the database we want to search (the smaller database search will process faster).

A search on the term "pregnancy" found over 1700 items, and gave us a digest of the first 10 results. These included Network News items, Web sites, and on-line medical journal items. The index is hyperlinked, and accessing the information from your search is easy; just click on the links. You may be able to see

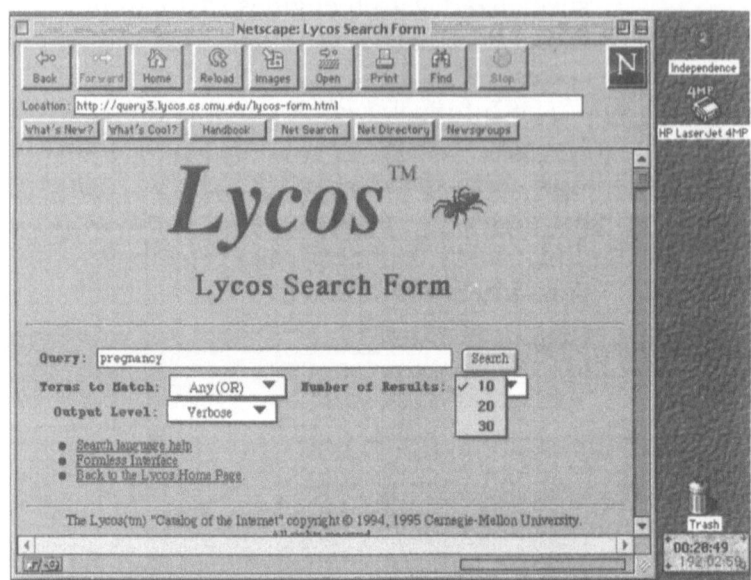

FIGURE 6.19.
Lycos WebCrawler
search options page.

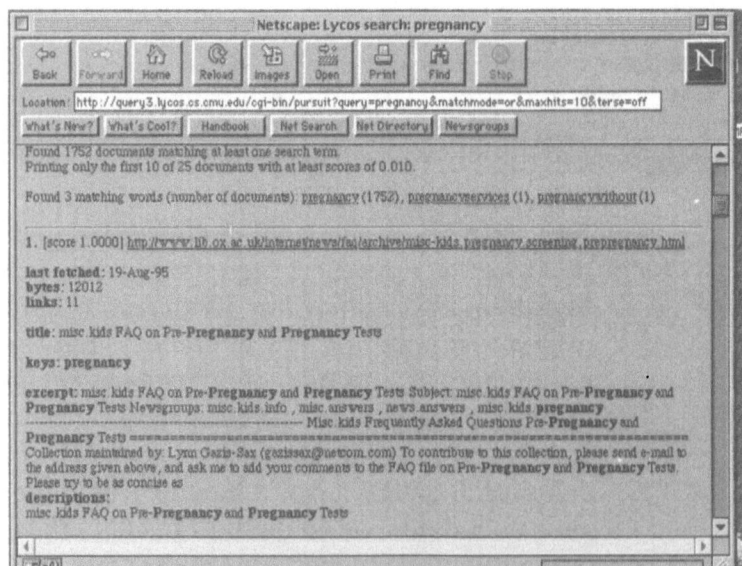

FIGURE 6.20.
Lycos search
results on the term
"pregnancy."

some information on the contents at the link here as well, as Lycos captures keywords and short descriptions.

You may also want to look at the WebCrawler at the University of Washington. This search engine works like Lycos, and also delivers a hypertext list of results. You can configure the search parameters by using drop-down lists, and there's also on-line help.

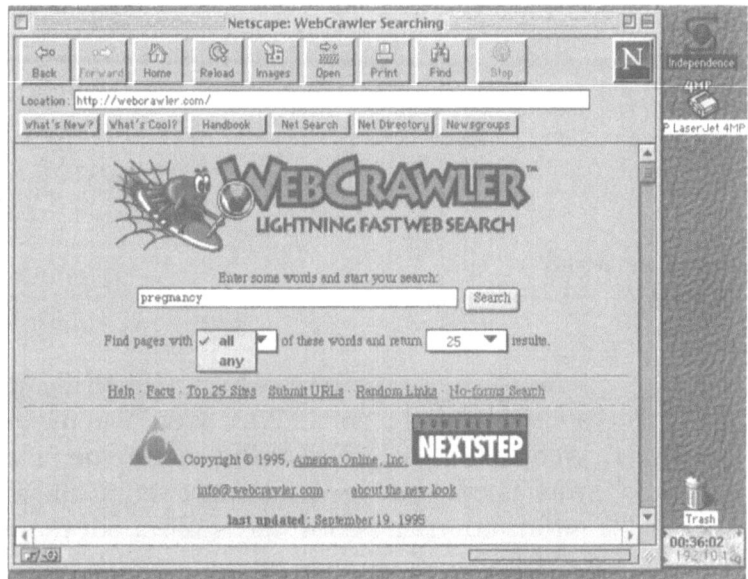

FIGURE 6.21.
The WebCrawler
home page.

Our search on the subject "pregnancy" found over 295 references and returned the first 25, in a numbered list weighted according to the relative appearance of our term.

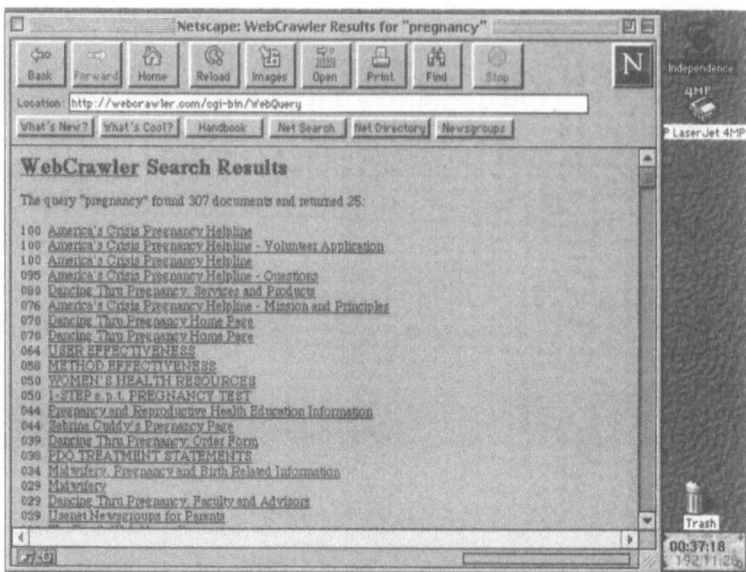

FIGURE 6.22.
WebCrawler results for the term "pregnancy."

You can use these search engines to glean information on any source from the World Wide Web. You may have to weed out the Web sources you find at the end of your search to see if they fit your needs, but you'll be surprised at the amount and depth of information on almost any subject out there.

7
Files on the Net and
Great Mac Web Sites

There are a great many Mac files on the Internet, including the
helper applications you'll need to get the most out of Netscape,
interesting applications, games and font collections, and official
Apple software updates.

Web Sites for Mac Software

Apple's home page on the Web (at `http://www.apple.com`) has
links to official Apple software archives, including system utilities and upgrades, as well as technical information, product data
sheets, and more. Go to the main site to find the links to the main
Apple shareware sites as well. (See Figure 7.1.)

Apple also has a Support and Information site you can go to
directly (`http://www.info.apple.com`). This site combines technical support and developer divisions, and is the main source for
software updates. You can also search the tech info library for
release notes and product information on new software available
here. (See Figure 7.2.)

This site links directly to `ftp.info.apple.com`. Just click on
the Software Updates selection, and you'll see an easy to navigate server in the standard Web hypertext format. There are sec-

FIGURE 7.1.
Apple's main Web
site.

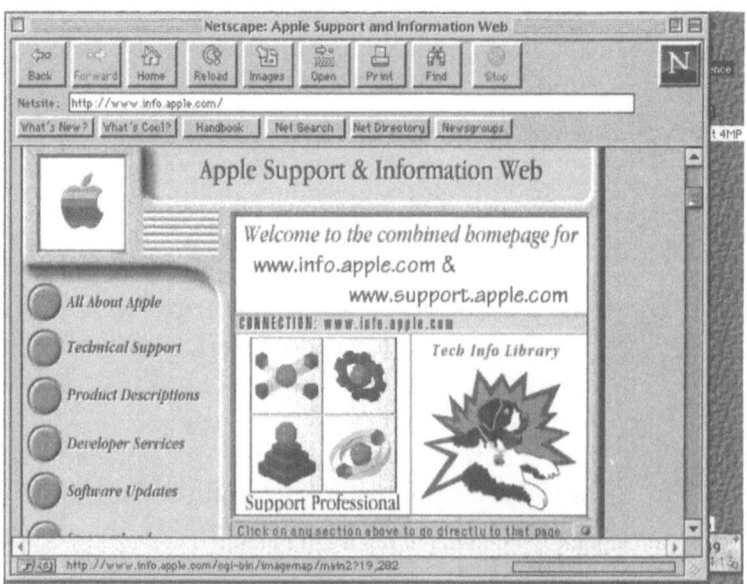

FIGURE 7.2.
Apple's Support and
Information Web.

tions for Mac software for displays and peripherals, networking and communications, printing, system software, and utilities. Use Netscape to view the .TXT files that accompany the binaries in these directories (just click on them, and Netscape will load them internally). Hold down the Option key and click on a file link name to have Netscape download it to your hard drive (this is the same technique you use to download any Mac software from an FTP directory or Web site). Note that the files for FTP sites are usually in the BinHex binary-to-text format, and compressed as well; you'll need the programs to decode and decompress the programs before you install them. A good all-around decoding and decompression program is Stuffit Expander; you can find shareware versions at Mac software FTP sites.

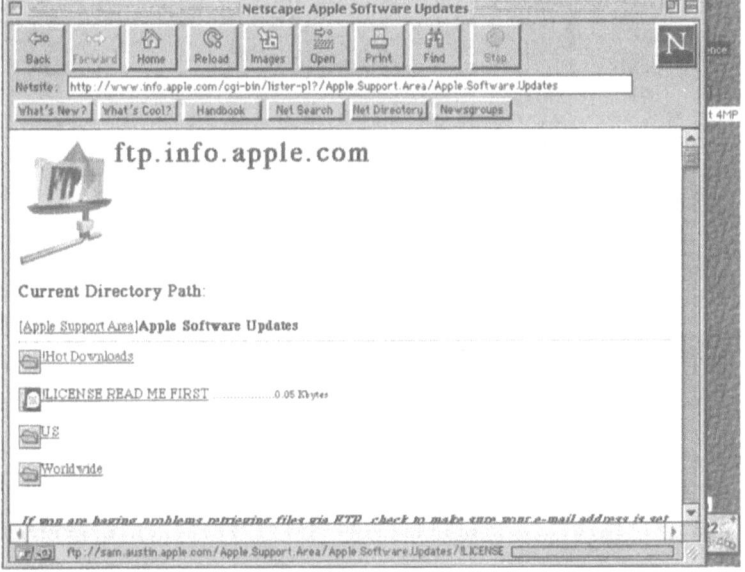

FIGURE 7.3.
FTP site for
Software Updates at
ftp.info.apple.com.

Apple has also made available a good mirror site for Mac shareware files from the primary archive sites at Stanford University (Info-Mac) and the University of Michigan. A mirror site is a server that replicates the contents of another site; this allows more users to access these computers without overloading them. The `mirror.apple.com` Web site has FTP interfaces to the same collections above, as well as a search engine you can use to look up software in the archives. (See Figures 7.4 and 7.5.)

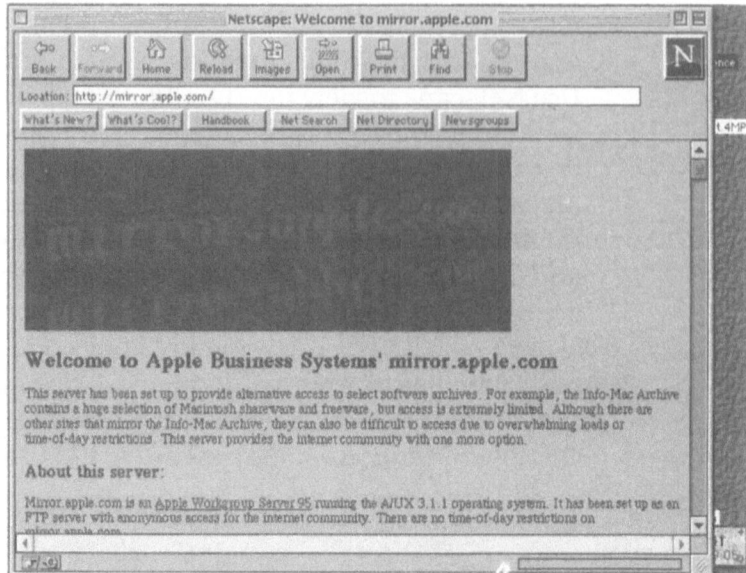

FIGURE 7.4.
The
mirror.apple.com
site at Apple.

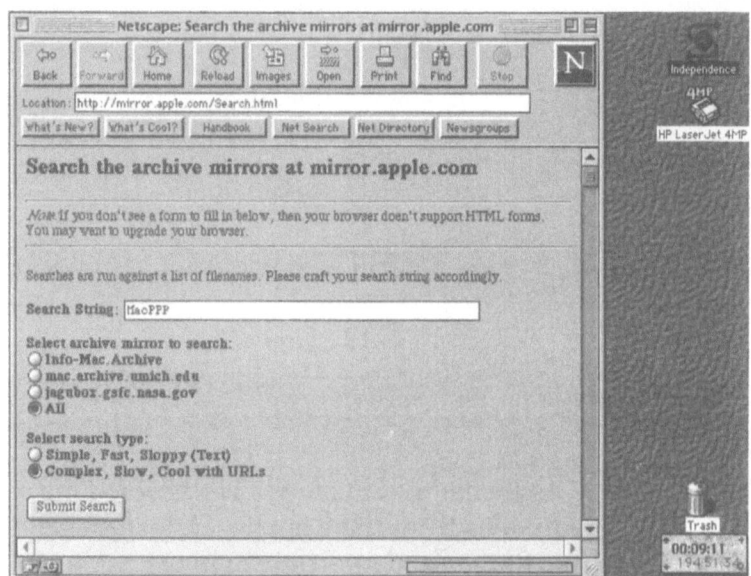

FIGURE 7.5.
The
mirror.apple.com
search page.

The mirror to Info-Mac shows a standard type of FTP server, viewable under Netscape as a series of file directories. All you have to do is click on the folders to move between them. Use Netscape's Back button to move back out of a folder.

InfoMac has a wide range of Mac software, including system

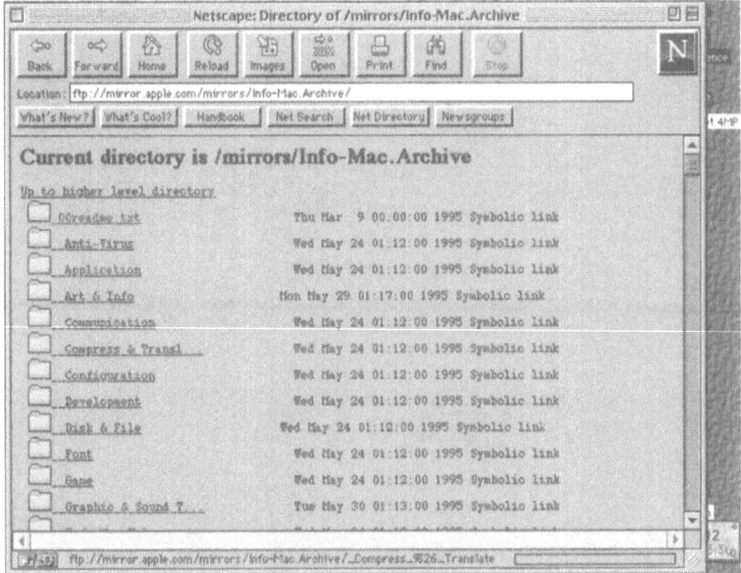

FIGURE 7.6.
The InfoMac FTP
server.

utilities, compression and translation software, applications, games, fonts, graphics and sound tools. There are also help files available. Click on the .TXT README files for more information about what's located in the current directory, and the associated text files paired to read about the programs before you download them. (See Figure 7.7.)

There are other mirror sites for InfoMac, as well as a CD-ROM that is updated periodically. Find the site closest to you geographically to reduce the demands you place on the Internet, and to allow you to connect more reliably. You can locate a mirror server near you by looking in the Help sections of the FTP servers you reach, or try the list at the Ultimate Macintosh site, http://www.freepress.com/myee/info-mac-mirrors.html.

You can search the InfoMac archives by using a number of Web-based utilities. The InfoMac HyperArchive at MIT includes a search panel at the main page (http://hyperarchive.lcs.mit.edu/HyperArchive.html), plus links to subject directories and abstracts of file contents. You can also get a reverse-chronological listing of files submitted to the archive, starting with the very last file uploaded to date. It's a powerful way to navigate the large number of files available at InfoMac. (See Figure 7.8.)

There are also searchable indices for the electronic digest reports of software recently made available at InfoMac. Check out

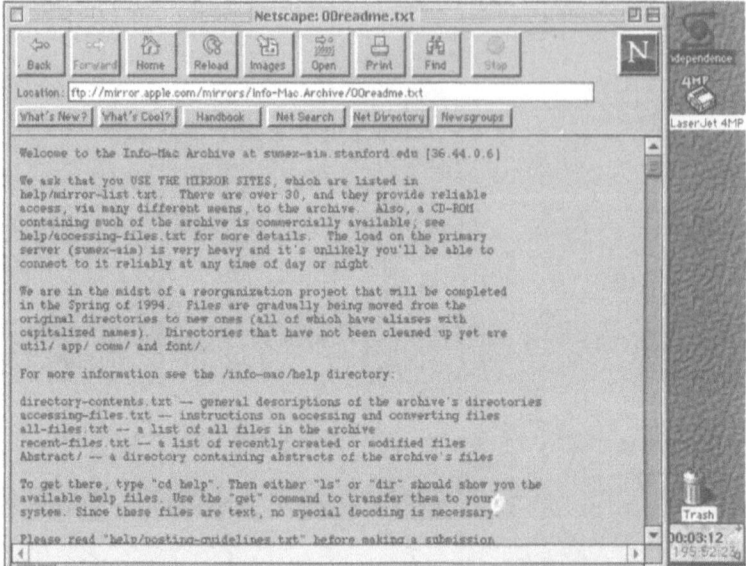

FIGURE 7.7.
A README file
from the InfoMac
archives.

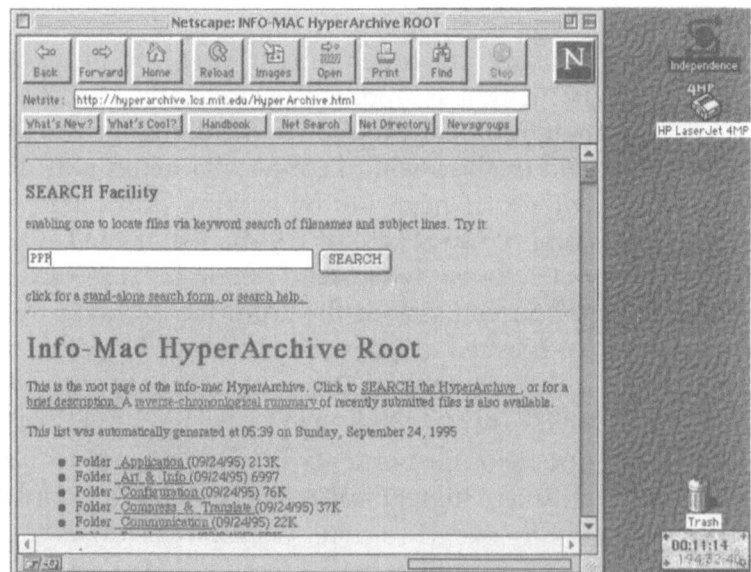

FIGURE 7.8.
The InfoMac
HyperArchive at MIT.

the MIDNet InfoMac site for more information. You can search the digests by title, keyword, and author. There's also a good set of information here about using the Info-Mac servers, and links to digest archives.

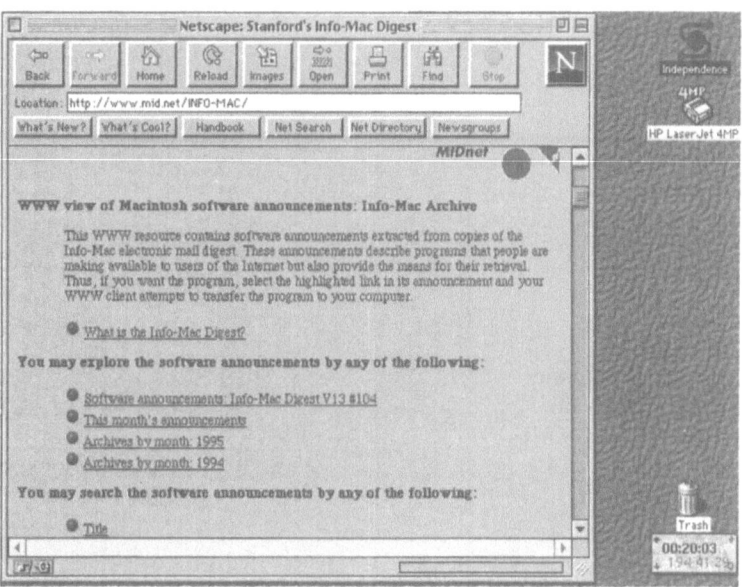

FIGURE 7.9.
The MIDNet InfoMac site.

You can also reach a mirror site for the University of Michigan MERIT archive of Mac software at mirror.apple.com. The FTP directory is set up in much the same way as the InfoMac archives. There's a lot of good software here, in categories ranging from graphics and sound utilities, hypercard stacks and related materials, development tools, and Power Macintosh–specific programs. (See Figure 7.10.)

There are HyperMedia Web sites with hypertext indices and search engines for the UMich Mac software site and its mirrors. These provide a good interface for Netscape users to the collection. The UBU index at Hahneman University (http://ubu.hahnemann.edu/UBUdex) is built up directly from the UMich archive site, and includes descriptions and links to files in a hypertext format. (See Figure 7.11.)

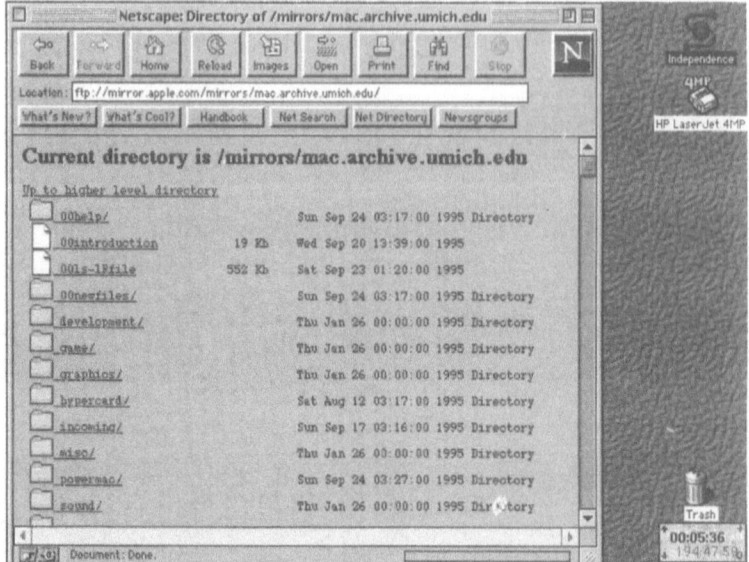

FIGURE 7.10.
The FTP directory at Apple's mirror site for the UMich MERIT site.

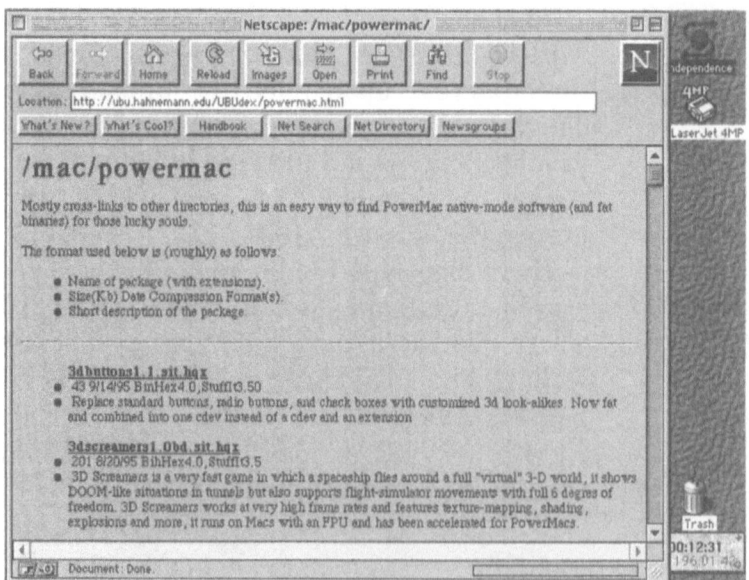

FIGURE 7.11.
The UBU index of the UMich FTP server /mac/powermac directory.

NEXOR, located in the United Kingdom, also offers an index to the UMich archive (`http://pubweb.nexor.co.uk/public/mac/archive/welcome.html`), which features a search panel you can use to look for files by their names and/or descriptions. You can also directly access the directories by subject, and view a list of recently added files.

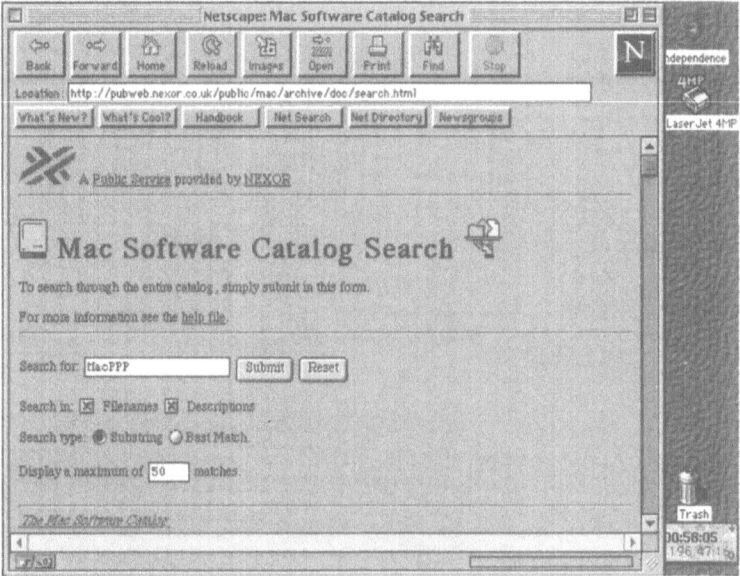

FIGURE 7.12.
The Mac software search engine at NEXOR for the UMich archive.

The UTexas archive site (`http://wwwhost.ots.utexas.edu`) is available with an interface totally designed with Netscape and Web browsers in mind. Categories include applications, communications, Internet software, compression utilities, graphics and sound programs, and games. There's also a good section on system software, including extensions and control panels. While this site doesn't have as many files as Info-Mac or the UMich sites, it's well maintained. You can find current versions of useful software here, in an easy-to-navigate format. Each entry includes a full explanation of the associated file, and there are also indices you can browse by product type, author, and date released.

For a large search engine that can look at the main Mac archives and lead you to the nearest places to download the files in them, try the Virtual Shareware Library at C/Net Central. You can also look at lists of the most popular downloads and new arrivals. The search results also include feedback on the reliability of a particular downloading site. (See Figure 7.14.)

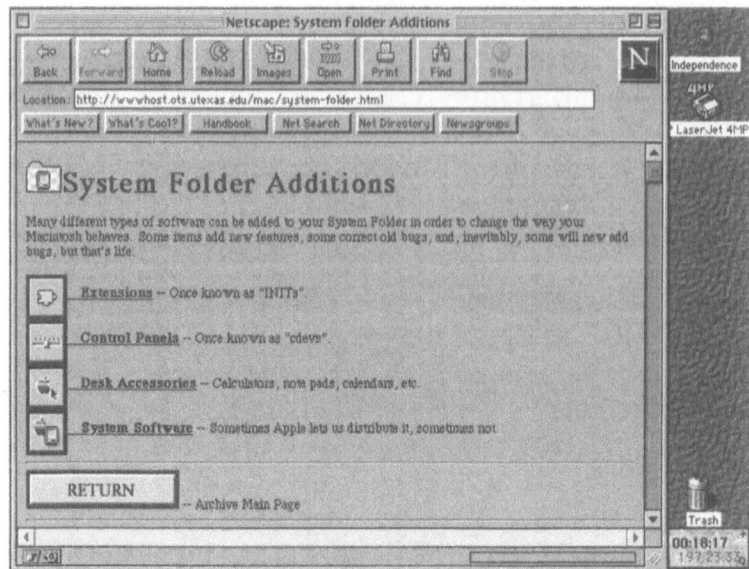

FIGURE 7.13.
The UTexas Mac software archive System Software section.

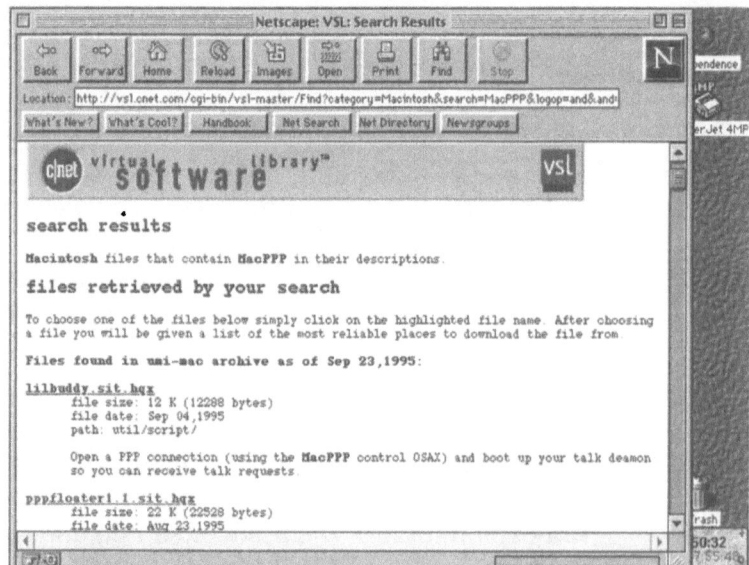

FIGURE 7.14.
The Virtual Shareware Library results for a Macintosh search on the term "MacPPP."

You also might want to look at a large list of Mac FTP sites with links in hypertext format at `http://rever.nmsu.edu/~bgrubb/mac-ftp-list.html`. The Mac-FTP-List also includes information on FTP site status. Look for interesting places like `ftp://seeding.apple.com`, a development site from Apple.

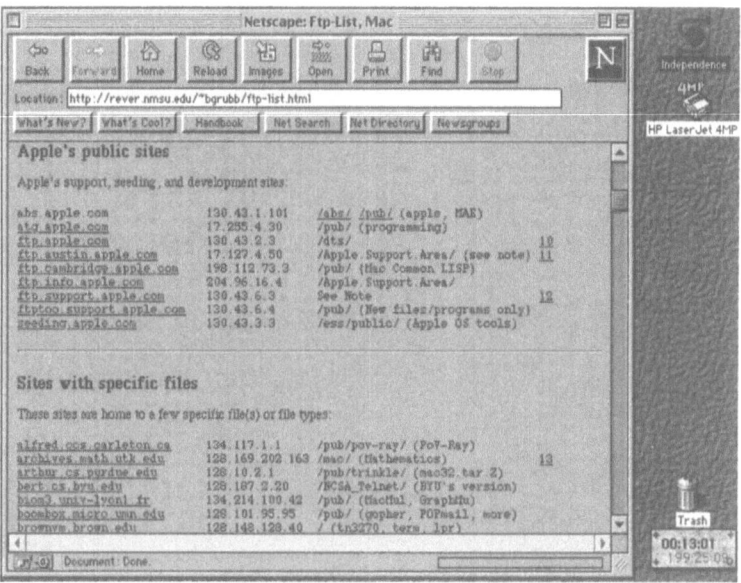

FIGURE 7.15.
The Mac-FTP-List, showing partial listings.

Be sure to make a stop at Michael Yee's ULTIMATE Mac page (`http://www.freepress.com/myee/umac.html`) to find links to all kinds of Mac software, including sections leading to Mac shareware archives, game sites, and Internet software locations. There is also a great list of companies that have Web and FTP sites of their own. You can usually find software at a particular vendor's site that may include the latest program upgrades, as well as downloadable product descriptions and pictures, and even some Web-based on-line ordering systems you can use to buy software directly from the manufacturer. (See Figure 7.16.)

The Well-Connected Mac site (`http://www.macfaq.com`) can also give you a good guide to what's out there for Macintosh, including a downloadable bookmark file you can use with Netscape with links to Mac vendor sites. Look at the CyberRESOURCES (`http://www.neo-logic.com/neo-logic/CyberResources.html`, under Mac resources) list, and pro-Macintosh sites called MacMania (`http://www.europa.com/~bubba/mac/appleindex.html`),

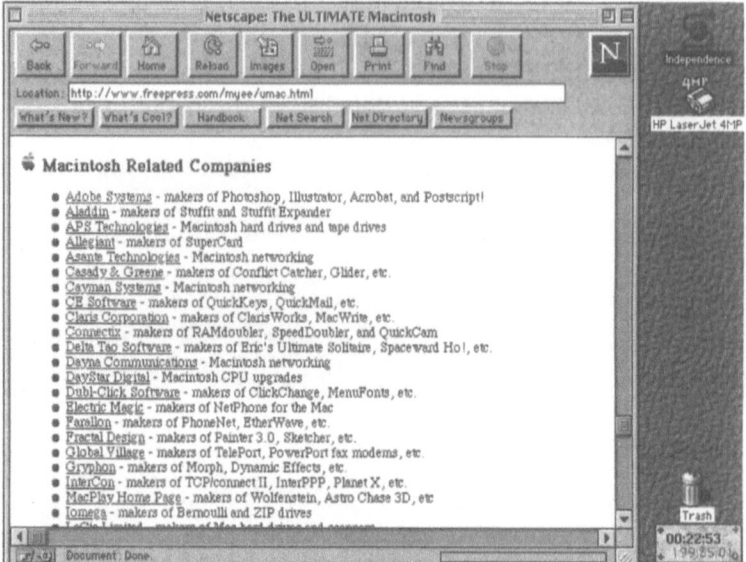

FIGURE 7.16.
The ULTIMATE Mac site's list of links to Mac-related companies on the Web.

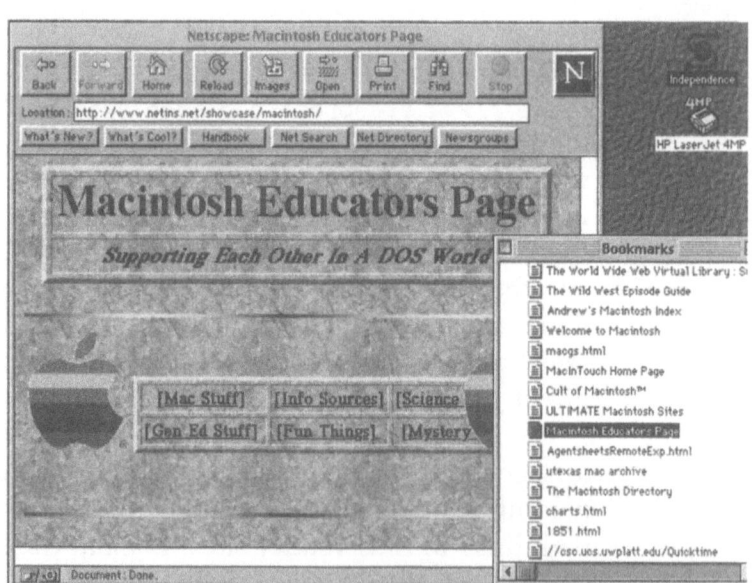

FIGURE 7.17.
The Macintosh Educators Page.

MacInTouch (`http://www.ultranet.com/~ricford/`), The Macintosh Directory (`http://pogo.wright.edu.mac/mac.html`), and Welcome To Macintosh (`http://astro.nwu.edu/lentz/mac/home-mac.html`). Teachers may be interested in looking at the Macintosh Educators Page (`http://www.netins.net/showcase/macintosh`) for more useful links and information.

There are also a number of sites directly related to the Powerbook, including the Official Powerbook Home Page (`http://flash.lakeheadu.ca/dmwadson/PB_Home_Pages/PowerBook_Home.html`) and the wonderful Powerbook Army (`http://hisurf.aloha.com/PBA/index.html`) site. These include links to helpful utilities and updated system software as well.

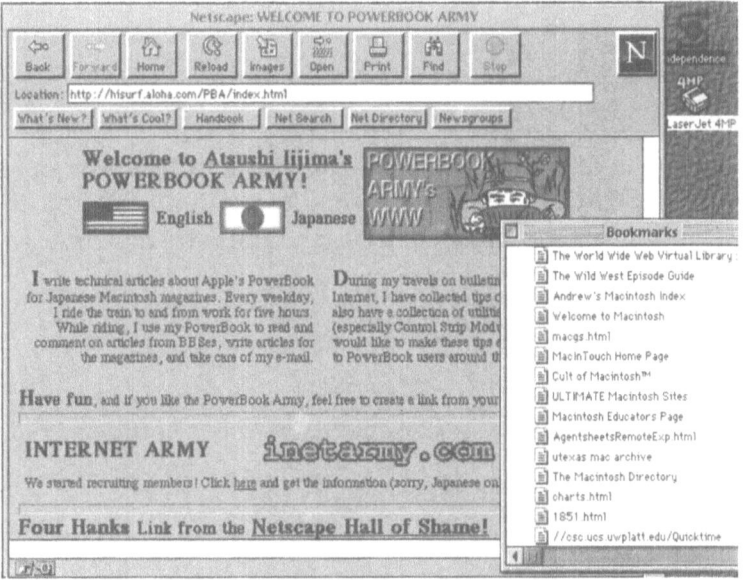

FIGURE 7.18.
The PowerBook
Army home page.

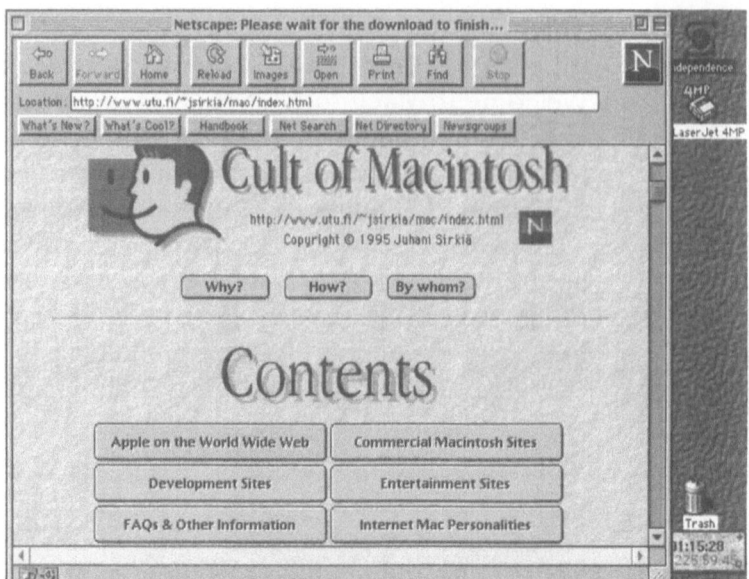

FIGURE 7.19.
The Cult of
Macintosh Web site.

Finally, take a look at the Cult of Macintosh for a particularly well-designed Web site of things related to the Mac. It's got a good Mac feel to it, and the information is well arranged. Find it at http://www.utu.fi/~jsirkia/mac/.

8
On-Line Magazines, Journals, and Books

The Internet is a great source for on-line magazines, journals, and books. Several different types are obtainable, from basic text formats to interactive Web documents. Netscape makes it easy to access all of these from its intuitive interface. Mac users have an especially good selection of on-line publications centered just on Mac topics.

Macintosh-Specific Magazines on the World Wide Web

The MacWorld site (www.macworld.com) is a very well designed on-line version of the Mac monthly. You can read the same articles here, including features, columns, reviews, and buyers' guides. Special Web features include columns on the Internet, including places to go to find good Net tools and related software, and an online advice section you can use to ask you own questions. There are also discussion forums and searchable back issue archives.

MacWEEK's Web site is where you can find investigative-type news, comparative reviews, and feature articles about the Mac and Apple in general. You can get the full text of current issues online at http://www.zdnet.com/~macweek. The on-line edition

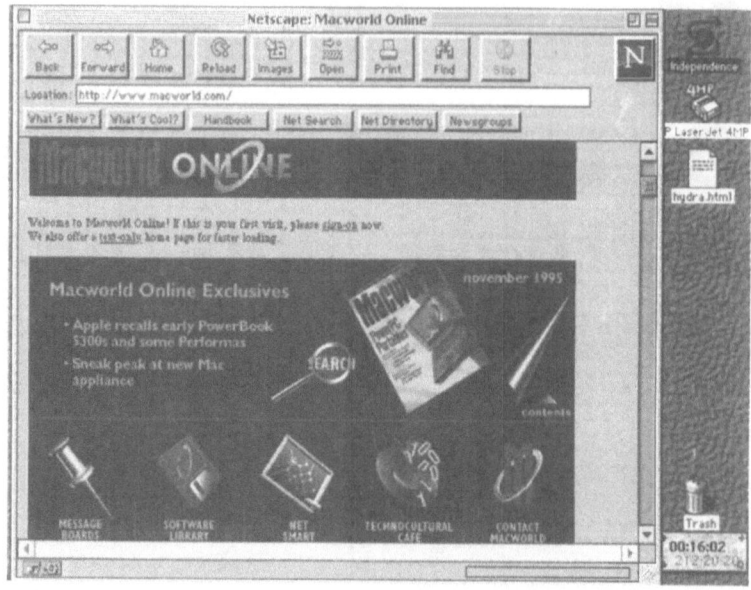

FIGURE 8.1.
The MacWorld Web site.

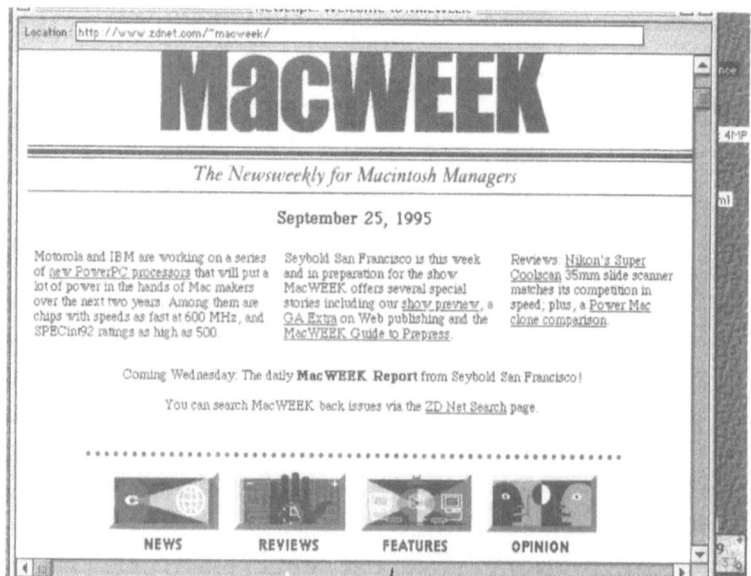

FIGURE 8.2.
The *MacWEEK* Web site.

also includes exclusive reports not available in the print edition, and easy-to-use archives with links to past weekly issues.

MacUser's Web site (`http://www.zdnet.com/~macuser/`) has a good collection of monthly articles from the Mac magazine, including reviews, features, and regular columnists. There are also sections devoted to on-line publishing, hands-on help, and games. You'll also find a back issue index here, and a link to a large NetMap of interesting sites.

FIGURE 8.3.
The MacUser Web site.

TidBITS is another electronic Mac information resource you won't want to miss. This weekly features the latest news, views, and reviews about the Macintosh and how it fits into the greater world of the personal computer. It's very up-to-date, and the on-line versions include links to the story subjects and software reviewed. Find the issues at `http://www.dartmouth.edu/pages/TidBITS/TidBITS.html`, and the main TidBITS home page at `http://king.tidbits.com`. (See Figure 8.4.)

You may also find Apple's *Information Alley* useful (`http://www.info.apple.com/info.alley/info.alley.html/`). This is an on-line support magazine for Apple customers, with articles on software and hardware issues, user tips and techniques, and technical issues. Articles are available to download in Acrobat and Common Ground format for off-line reading. (See Figure 8.5.)

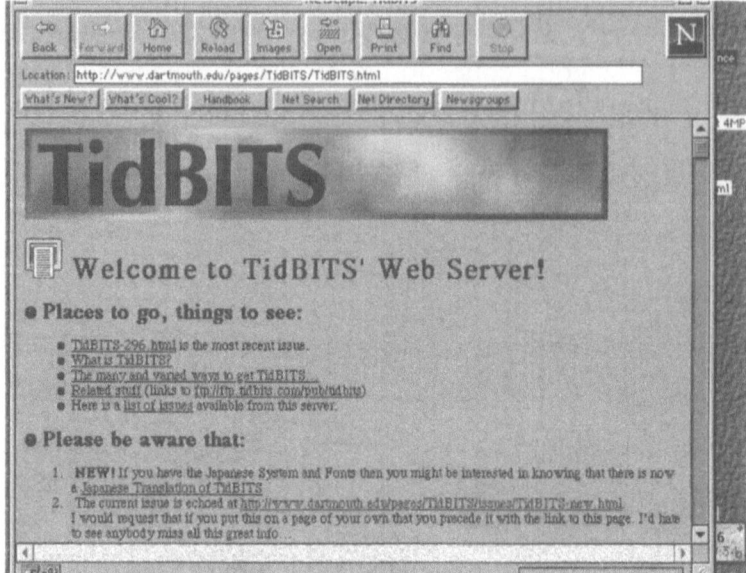

FIGURE 8.4.
A sample issue of
the *TidBITS* Web
magazine.

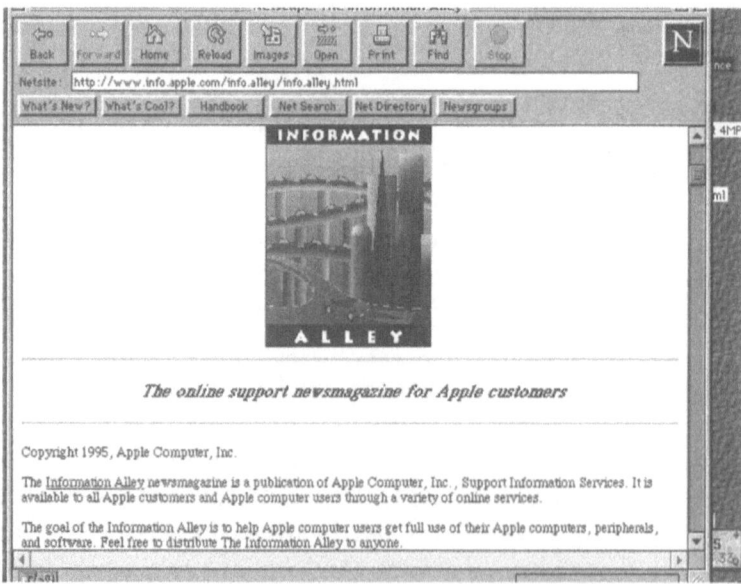

FIGURE 8.5.
Apple's *Information
Alley*.

MacTech's site (`http://www.mactech.com`) caters to the Apple development community. It features over 1500 pages of information, including developer articles, programming FAQs, job listings, and development tools file archives.

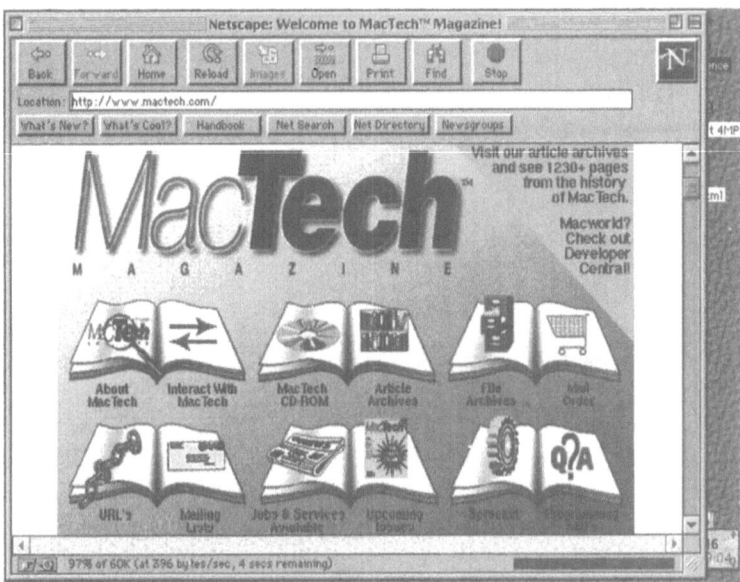

FIGURE 8.6.
MacTech's Web site.

Apple also has a developer publication on the Web, called *develop*. The on-line version offers selected articles from the subscription-based Apple Technical Journal, including programming techniques and related features. The articles are also available in Common Ground (with a built-in viewer) or Acrobat format for off-line reading, and the on-line versions also have sample code you can download. Look for *develop* at `http://www.info.apple.com/dev/developtoc.html`. (See Figure 8.7.)

General-Interest Magazines

The range of general-interest magazines presented on the Web is wide, ranging from scientific journals to art and architecture magazines, history journals, and literature. Publishing electronically has opened up a means of expression for a lot of people who otherwise would not have this outlet. This makes reading electronic journals a rewarding and refreshing experience. You

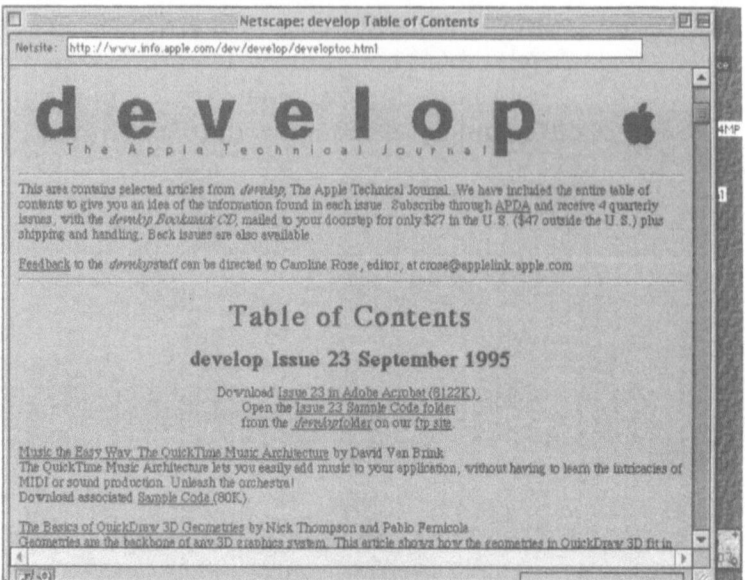

FIGURE 8.7.
The *develop* journal
on the Web.

should note that some of the magazines available over the Web are in text format, more like Gopher servers than Web pages. Netscape can handle these well, however, and you shouldn't have any trouble viewing them with your Macintosh.

To get started with electronic journals, take advantage of the many good indices established on the Internet. The Yahoo Directory has good listings for magazine in nearly all of its subject headings.

CERN, The Institute for Particle Physics in Switzerland, has developed the Virtual Library, a Web catalog of links to particular subjects (`http://www.w3.org/pub/DataSources/bySubject/Overview.html`).

Go to the topic for Electronic Journals, and you'll see a further index page, with a comprehensive list of journals and magazines. (See Figure 8.10.)

There are a number of interesting items listed, and the index is dynamic; it should continue to be updated regularly. You'll also find pointers to other electronic journal indices on the Internet here, and a helpful search tool. (See Figure 8.10.)

You should also note that many of the journals and magazines listed are actually part of collections on Gopher servers. Gophers are a good way to index text (like on-line magazine and journals), and are easily accessible for users with slower connections.

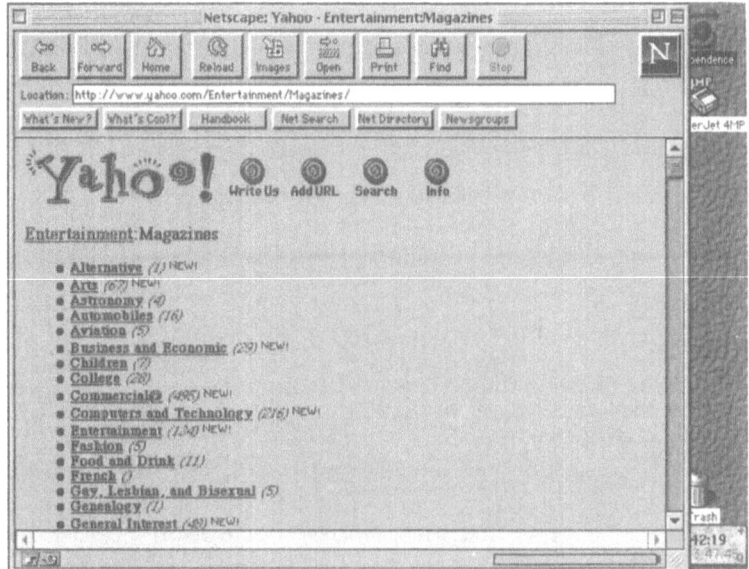

FIGURE 8.8.
The Yahoo
Directory's listings
for magazines.

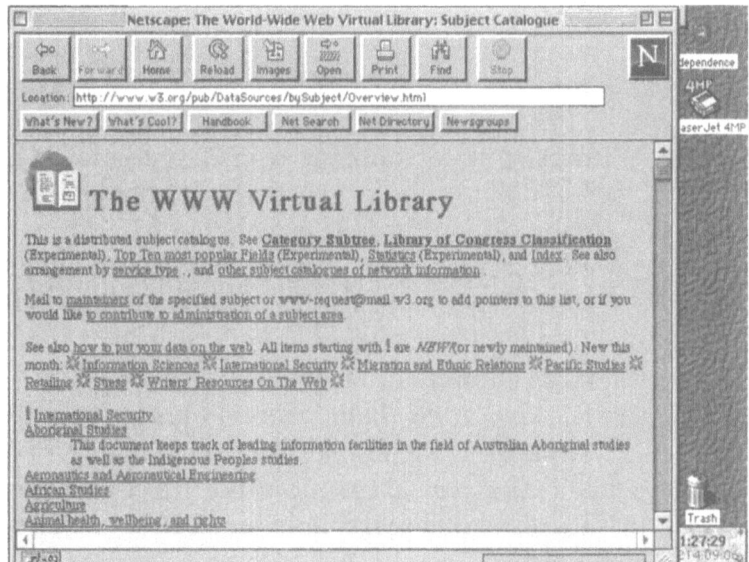

FIGURE 8.9.
The opening page for
the Virtual Library
index at CERN.

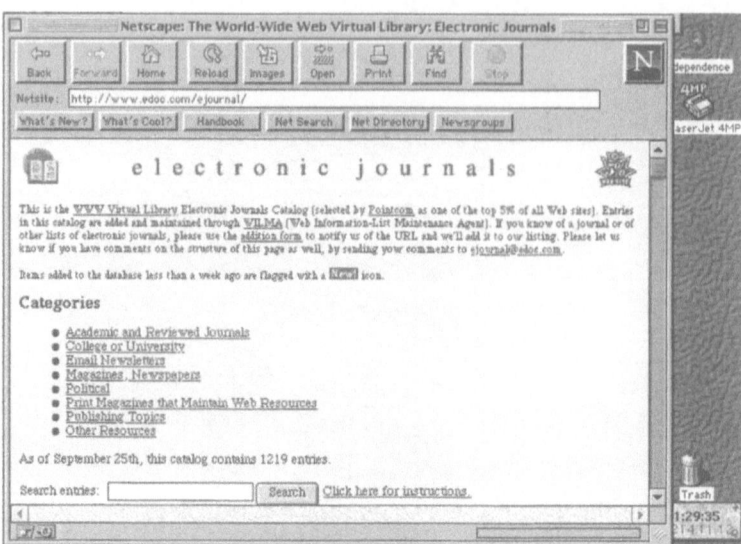

FIGURE 8.10.
Electronic Journals
index at the Virtual
Library, opening
page.

The Authors, Books, Periodicals, and Zines area at the WELL (Whole Earth 'Lectronic Link) is a public-access gopher with a wide range of interesting topics, including texts from William S. Burroughs and Bruce Sterling, electronic information from magazines like *Mondo 2000*, and specialty items like the Factsheet Five reviews of eclectic smaller magazines and an AIDSwire Digest archive. Use Netscape to go to the WELL gopher area at `http://gopher.well.sf.ca.us:70/1/Publications/`, or follow the links for the WELLgopher at `www.well.com`.

The Electronic Newsstand, at `gopher.enews.com`, provides mostly small samples from larger magazines, including Table of Contents and trial articles. It's not a total electronic magazine solution, but it does provide a taste of the magazines featured. Representative articles from magazines like *Business Week*, *Multimedia World*, *Worth*, *Travel Holiday*, *The Sporting News*, and *The Literary Review* show a good range of topics. Sample material from computer magazines like *CADENCE*, *Virtual Reality World*, *PC Novice*, *PC Today*, and *Computerworld*, as well as from mainstream magazines like the *New Yorker*, *Air & Space/Smithsonian*, and *Discover*, rounds out the Electronic Newsstand's offerings. It's also got a searchable index to its articles.

Other Gophers for electronic journals are located at the University of Delaware (`gopher://morris.lib.udel.edu:70`) and the University of California at Santa Cruz, which features an index of

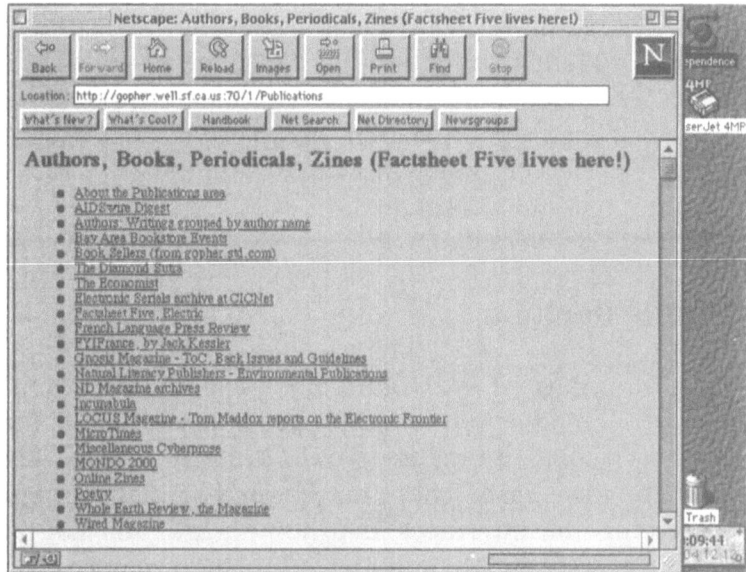

FIGURE 8.11.
The WELLgopher
Authors, Books,
Periodicals, and
Zines page.

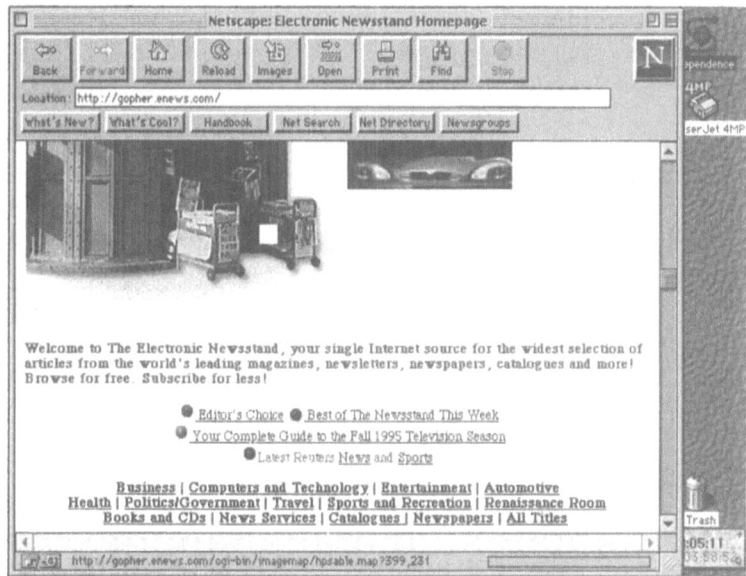

FIGURE 8.12.
The Electronic
Newsstand.

the extensive MELVYL library catalog, at gopher://scilibx.ucsc.edu:70/1 (also look in the Library section of this gopher for links to more electronic journals and magazines). You'll need to have Telnet configured for Netscape as an external program to reach some of the materials available from these Gopher servers. Look in the main Mac shareware archives for Telnet programs for Macintosh; they will work automatically with your PPP connection in most cases.

Beyond Gophers

Beyond the Gopher text-based interfaces, Netscape-style hyper-media Web versions have been developed for a number of magazines, along the lines of the ones that we've described that cover the Mac. These are easier to navigate, using the same hyper-link interfaces as a home page, and can also be formatted to present their information more clearly. Most also include advanced graphics and sound capabilities that cater well to the Macs' native strengths.

A good index to Web-based magazines is the E-Zines list at http://www.middlebury.edu/~otisg/zines.shtml. It's in an alphabetical format with annotations and direct links to full Web-based magazines. This includes magazines that have current newsstand versions, as well as Net-spawned zines that have only just arrived.

If you have a scientific bent, you might want to look at a list of the biology and medical journals available on the Net, in a list located at Harvard University. The http://golgi.harvard.edu/journals.html site (part of the WWW Virtual Library) includes links to peer-reviewed journals and extracts from the journals themselves, as well as newspapers, newsletters, and discussion groups.

The English Server at Carnegie-Mellon University (http://english-www.hss.cmu.edu) is a very well laid out gateway to a large amount of information on the humanities. Subject areas include art and architecture journals, drama, fiction, film and TV works, and newspapers/newsletters on many different topics. You can perform Gopher searches, link to hypermedia journals, and even leave mail for editors at the site (Figs. 8.15 and 8.16).

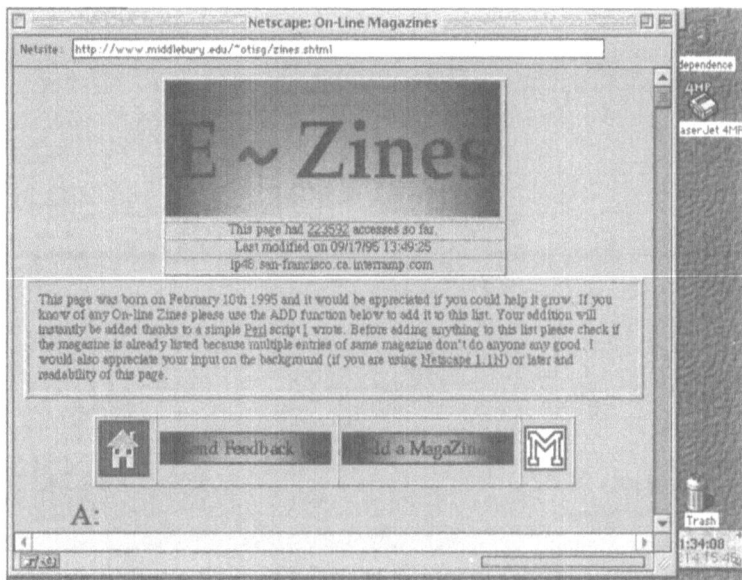

FIGURE 8.13.
The E-Zines list.

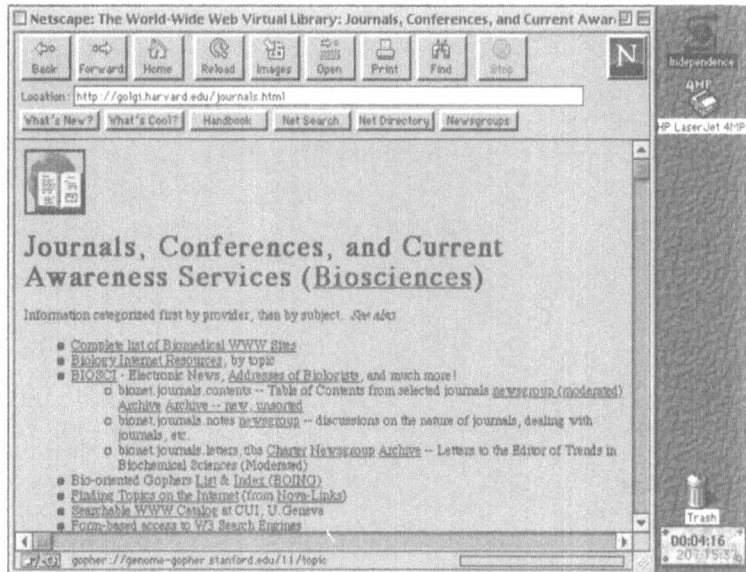

FIGURE 8.14.
The Biology and
Medical Journals
index at Harvard
University.

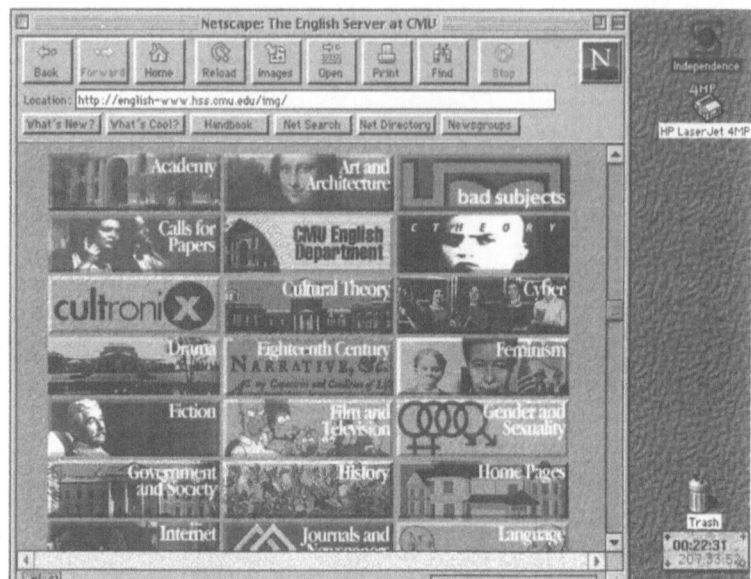

FIGURE 8.15.
The English Server
at Carnegie-Mellon
University.

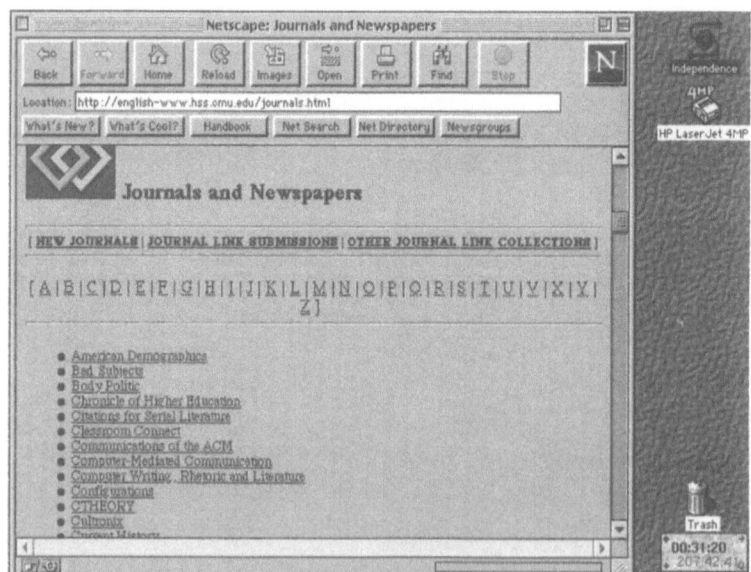

FIGURE 8.16.
The English Server
Journals and
Newspapers index.

Individual Web Browser Magazines and Books

One of the most interesting natural developments following the creation of Netscape and Web browsers in general has been the generation of interactive magazines and books. These can include stylized graphics, animations, and sound, as well as links to other Web sites and interactive elements like feedback via Email. There are cutting-edge periodicals like avant-garde student productions, as well as major mainstream publications like *Mother Jones* and *Time* magazine, in a rich hypermedia formats.

WORD (http://www.word.com) has a good mix of articles, including investigative reports, cultural discussions, and satire. The strong visual format may put a strain on some systems, but this magazine really shows off the power of the Web and browsers like Netscape.

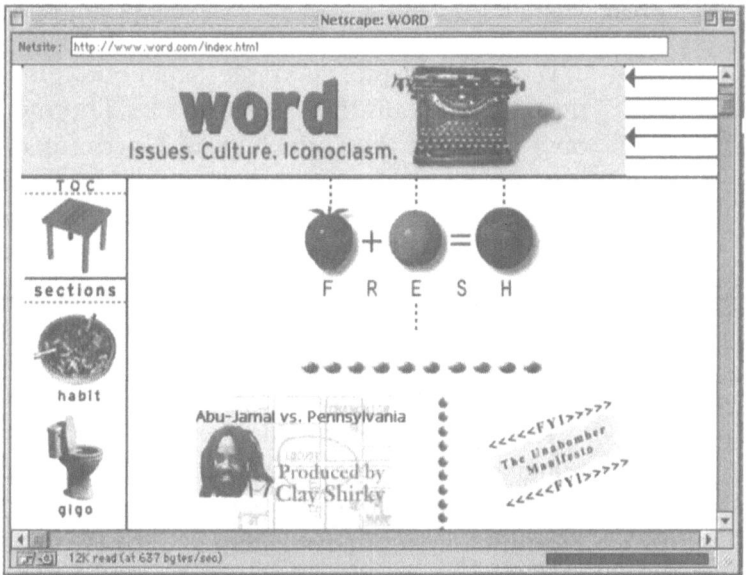

FIGURE 8.17.
WORD magazine.

Also check out *Buzznet*, for another example of a Web-based magazine with strong graphics and good original content. Find it at http://www.buzznet.net/buzznet.

Departure From Normal is a fun art journal that shows the capabilities of the Web to good effect. One of its recent issues featured a QuickTime movie in addition to text-based works. You can get there directly at: http://www.teleport.com/~xwinds/dfn.html.

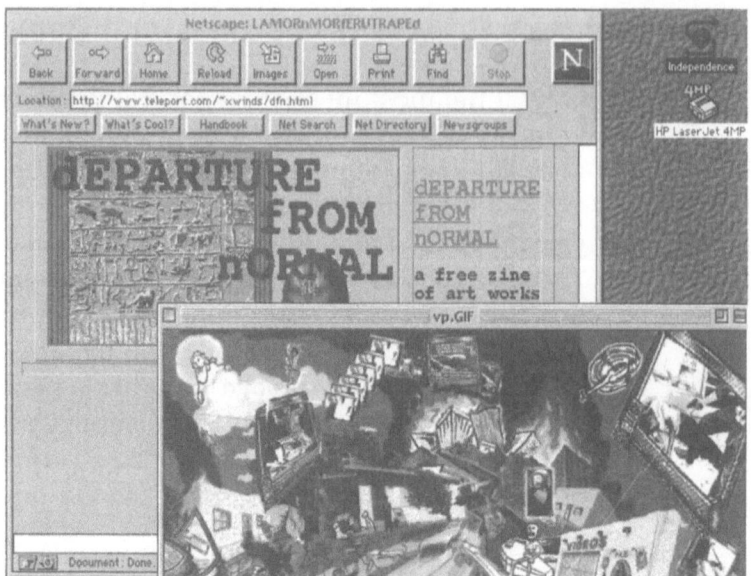

FIGURE 8.18.
Departure From Normal Table of Contents, with an external image being viewed.

Verbiage, despite its name, is a good collection of original fiction available on-line. It's edited by Thomas Boutell and located on a server at the University of North Carolina, and it seems to be a stable place for original literature on the World Wide Web. Check it out at `http://sunsite.unc.edu/boutell/verbiage`.

The smaller eclectic magazines are also worth checking out, if you can find them. The *Proust Said That!* on-line magazine, at `http://www.well.com/user/vision/proust/`, is an in-depth look at the 19th-century French writer. It includes short stories, background information, and even recipes.

The larger-scale magazine efforts on the Web include a full hypermedia version of *Mother Jones*, *Wired* magazine's *HotWired* Web site, and *Time Interactive* (Pathfinder). These are all good versions of on-line magazines, with World Wide Web interfaces and varying degrees of sophistication.

Mother Jones' HTML version is straightforward and clean, and shows up well under Netscape. It includes full-text articles with graphics, news commentary, and a Live Wire on-line discussion area. The **MOJO** Wire is at `http://www.mojones.com`. (See Figure 8.21.)

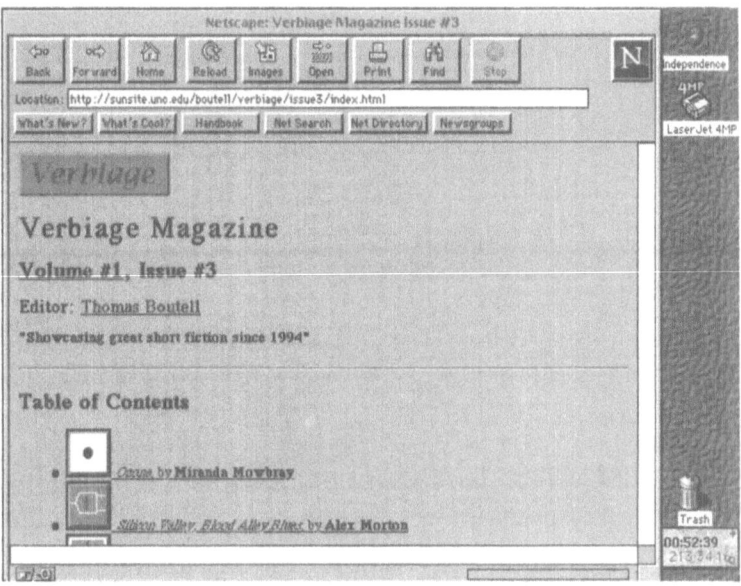

FIGURE 8.19.
Verbiage fiction
magazine.

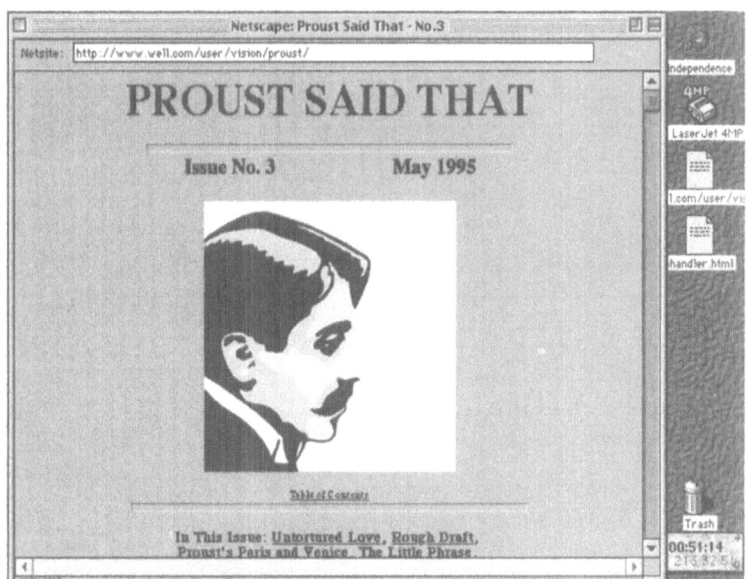

FIGURE 8.20.
Proust Said That!
magazine.

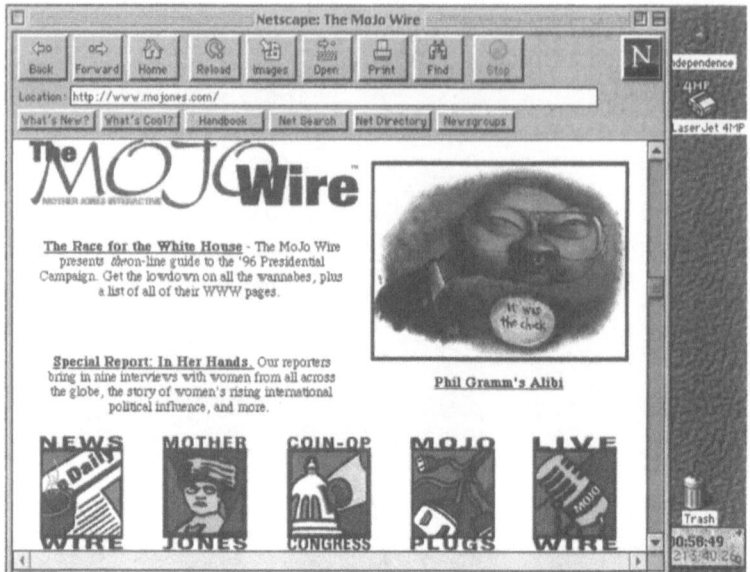

FIGURE 8.21.
An on-line issue of *Mother Jones* magazine.

HotWired, *Wired* magazine's reworking of parts of their magazine into a digital format, is an interesting proposition. There are good articles with graphics, sound, and animation files located here, and you may find something interesting in the on-line message forums. Try it yourself at: http://www.hotwired.com.

FIGURE 8.22.
The *HotWired* Web site.

The vast Time-Warner Internet site called Pathfinder is a good place to find slick magazines on the World Wide Web, including *Time* features and back issues, *Entertainment Weekly* reviews, and *Money* magazine advisories. Other divisions, like Time-Warner Publishing, are also represented. The offerings are well suited to the Web, including JPEG stills in the magazines and movie reviews and QuickTime previews of upcoming books and CD-ROMs. The Pathfinder system also includes messaging areas, like electronic bulletin boards. This is an opportunity to use the Time Web site like NetNews, though it's for local access. The Time universe is located at `http://www.pathfinder.com`.

FIGURE 8.23.
The *Time* magazine
Web site overview.

Playboy Enterprises has an on-line version of *Playboy* magazine available at `http://www.playboy.com`. The issues feature *Playboy* interviews with people like Bill Gates of Microsoft, not to mention the usual advice columns and downloadable Playmate photographs (Figure 8.24).

FIGURE 8.24.
Playboy Web site.

Books, Literature, and Miscellaneous

GNN Magazine, and a World Wide Web resource, is in its own category. The Global Network Navigator from O'Reilly and Associates is an attempt to provide a networked magazine to the Internet. It provides an electronic copy of *The Whole Internet Catalog* that's useful for navigating the Internet, and an on-line magazine, *WebReview*, that covers the World Wide Web. It also features a Best of the Net section and on-line magazines on topics like personal finance and travel. GNN is more heavily connected to the Internet than most on-line magazines, and has many useful links to a wide array of interesting sites. Get there directly at http://gnn.com.

The Daily Telegraph

The *Electronic Daily Telegraph*, an on-line version of the British newspaper, is a fine example of a graphics-intensive on-line newspaper. It features up-to-date news reports and editorial features, as well as full-color newswire photographs. For free registration, use the http://www.telegraph.co.uk address.

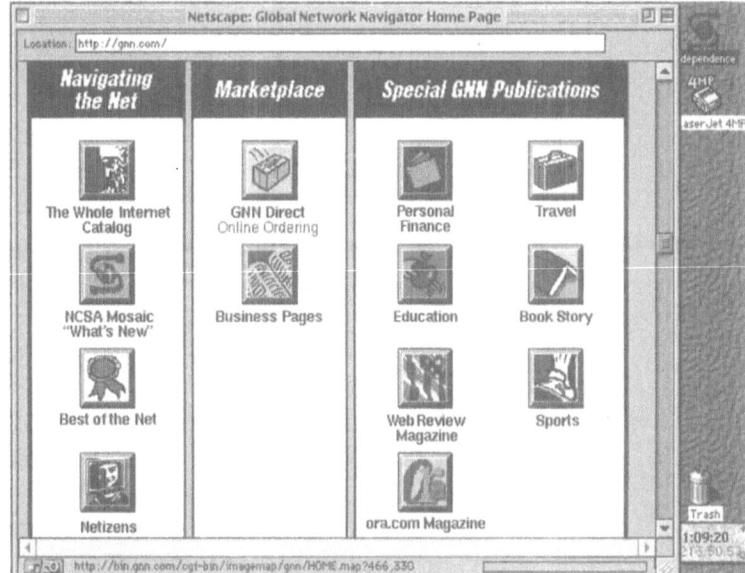

FIGURE 8.25. Representative offerings from O'Reilly and Associates' Global Network Navigator.

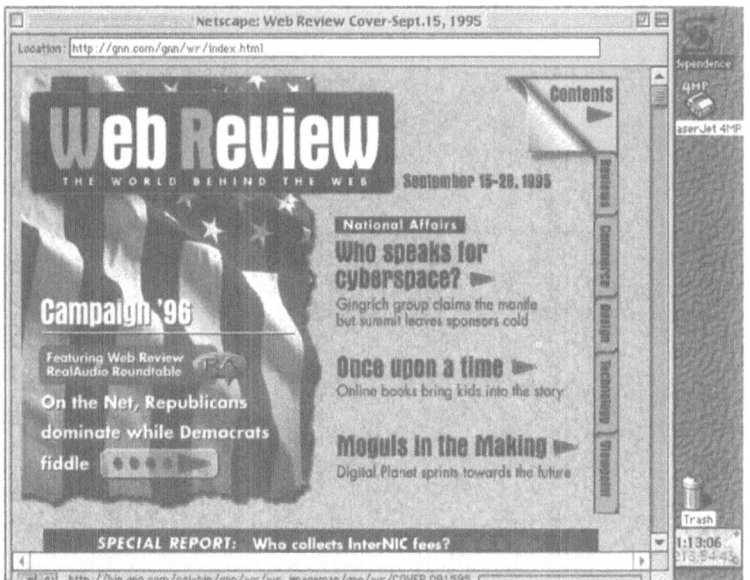

FIGURE 8.26. *WebReview* at gnn.com.

Project Gutenberg

Project Gutenberg is an ambitious, distributed Web project designed to put electronic books on-line. These range from basic downloadable text files to hypermedia documents that you can view with Netscape. HTML books available include fiction, featuring a lot of Edgar Rice Burroughs, Bram Stoker's *Dracula*, Mary Shelley's *Frankenstein*, Mark Twain's *The Adventures of Tom Sawyer*, and Melville's *Moby Dick*, among others. Essays and nonfiction includes Thomas Paine's *The Age of Reason*, the works of John Donne and St. John of the Cross, the collected Inaugural Addresses of the U.S. Presidents, Sun Tzu's *The Art of War*, and books on programming languages and book conservation. Poetry collections range from *Leaves of Grass* to the complete works of Wordsworth, and also include works by John Keats, Oscar Wilde, and Samuel Taylor Coleridge. Modern writing includes Hakim Bey's *Temporary Autonomous Zone* (poetic terrorism) and Philip Greenspun's *Travels with Samantha* (with color photos). Pointers to comprehensive lists of on-line works are located at the Project Gutenberg home page (`http://med-amsa.bu.edu/Gutenberg/Welcome.html`). You can also go directly to an alphabetical index at `http://med-amsa.bu.edu/Gutenberg/alpha.html`.

You can also find a good list of HTML Netscape-readable books at `http://www.cs.cmu.edu/Web/books.html`. There are close to a thousand works listed, and the number keeps growing every day. Search engines at this site can help you find a particular author or work, or you can browse the indices by subject. There are also links to servers with the collections of books themselves.

The Library of Congress Web site, located at `http://lcweb.loc.gov` is a must-see for people interested in a good on-line library source. It includes special exhibits that run under Mosaic Web browsers (for example, a recent selection included African-American culture, the voyage of Columbus, a tour of the Vatican library, and a view of the Dead Sea scrolls), select handbooks to worldwide countries, and links to the MARVEL and LOCIS on-line catalog systems. There are also sample pages for a proposed Global Electronic Library, with links to State, Local, and Federal World Wide Web sites, and a good collection of Internet resources and searchable indices.

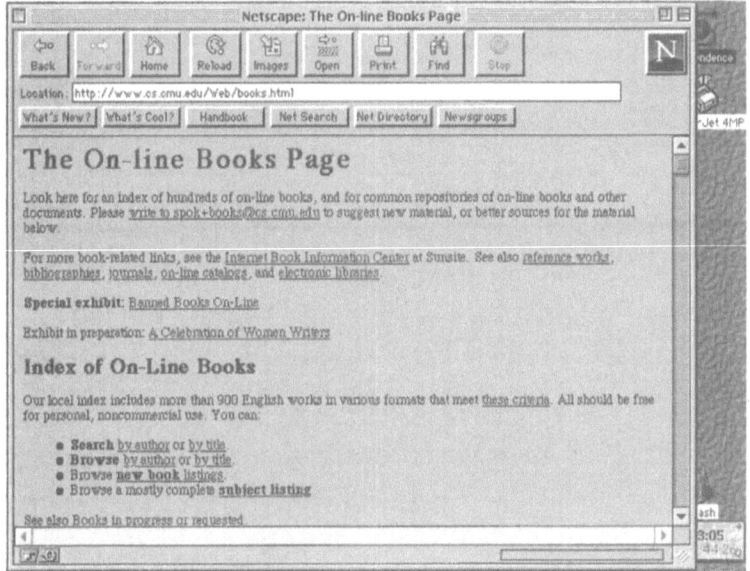

FIGURE 8.27.
CMU On-Line Books
Page.

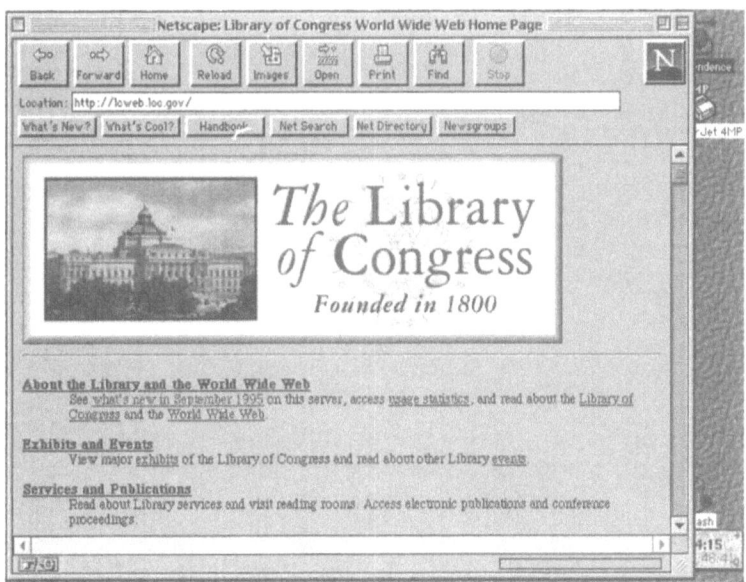

FIGURE 8.28.
The Library of
Congress Web site.

9
Art, Games, Music, and More

The World Wide Web is the home of many different types of artistic, intellectual, and fun pursuits, including on-line art galleries, comics-related home pages, music sites, and interactive games. There are also many different indices to this information available in formats that you can easily navigate in Netscape.

Art and Art Galleries

The art featured on the World Wide Web can be different from what you're used to seeing. It's a bit more freewheeling, loose, and inventive. The Netscape Web interface is used to good effect in these interactive types of artworks, however, so it's definitely worth a look. A good starting point is the ArtSource index at the University of Kentucky (`http://www.uky.edu/Artsource/artsourcehome.html`), which provides a comprehensive index to the art world on the Web.

The World Wide Arts Resource page has on-line artist and museum indices, links to publications and commercial arts resources, and a section on antiques. Find it at `http://www.concourse.com/wwar/`.

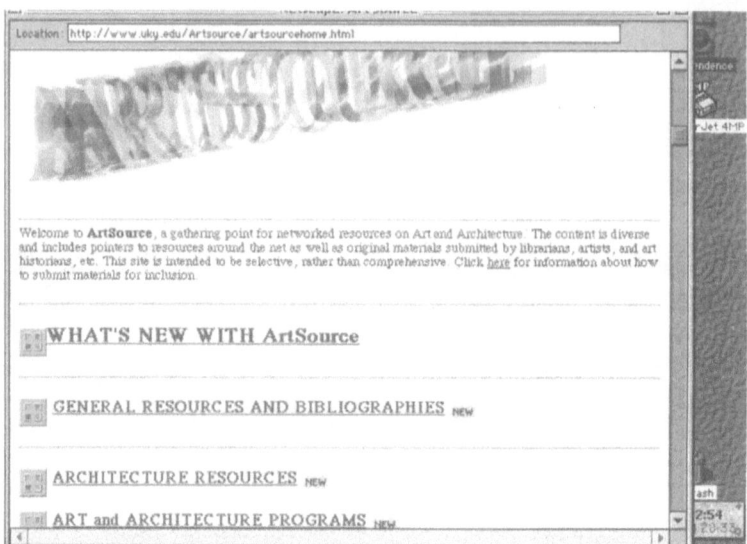

FIGURE 9.1.
The ArtSource home
page.

One museum to definitely visit on the Web is the WebMuseum
Network, formerly the WebLouvre, available in a good interactive
format tour from `http://sunsite.unc.edu/louvre` and a number of mirror sites. This site has a very nice collection of images
from various museums, including classic paintings, French me-
dieval artwork, and a tour of the city of Paris. It also includes
classical music sound files, video clips from French television,
and special exhibits.

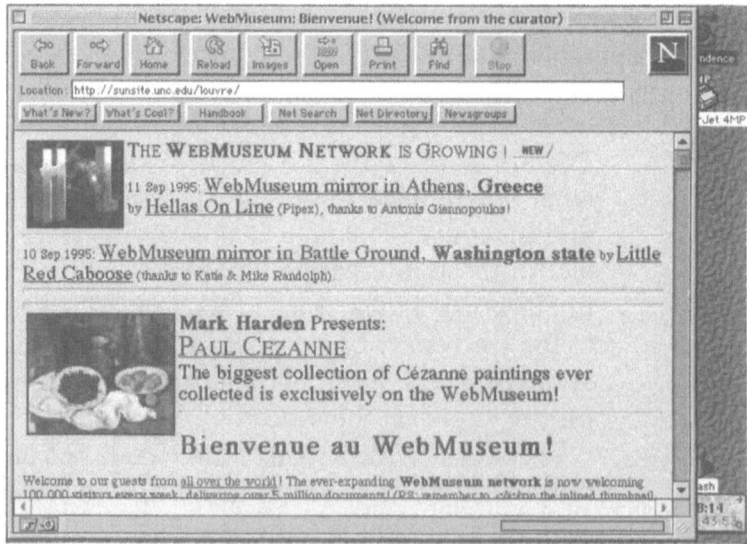

FIGURE 9.2.
The WebMuseum
Network.

The Virtual Library's Museums listings (at `http://www.comlab. ox.ac.uk/archive/other/museums.html`) are also worth browsing to find museums of many different types on the Internet. Try the Art listings as well (`http://info.cern.ch/hypertext/ DataSources/bySubject/Literature/Overview.html`).

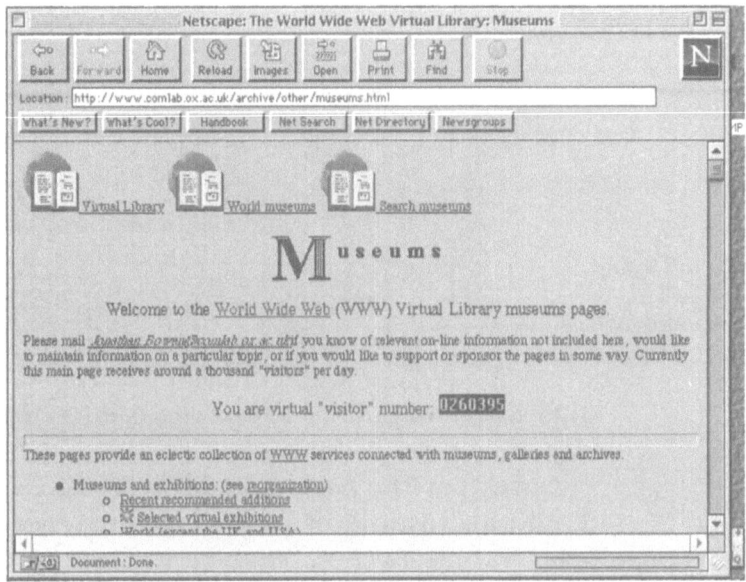

FIGURE 9.3.
The Virtual Library's
Museums page.

Other gallery collections include the School of Visual Arts in New York's "Cultural Difficulties," (`http://www.sva.edu/WGTB/ flypaper.html`), a collaborative exhibit consisting of art projects against censorship and links to related sites, and the (art)^n Laboratory at Northwestern University (`http://www.artn.nwu.edu`), featuring a Virtual Photography exhibit. (See Figure 9.4.)

Art exhibits and galleries on the World Wide Web change over time, so be sure to check the indices for current shows. Another good place to look for art information is on Yahoo, under the Art and Society and Culture sections. Use Netscape's Net Directory page to access those sections right from Netscape's home page.

Alternative Home Pages

The Internet is populated by people with a sense of humor, and an appreciation for the Arts. It's a rough sort of humor some-

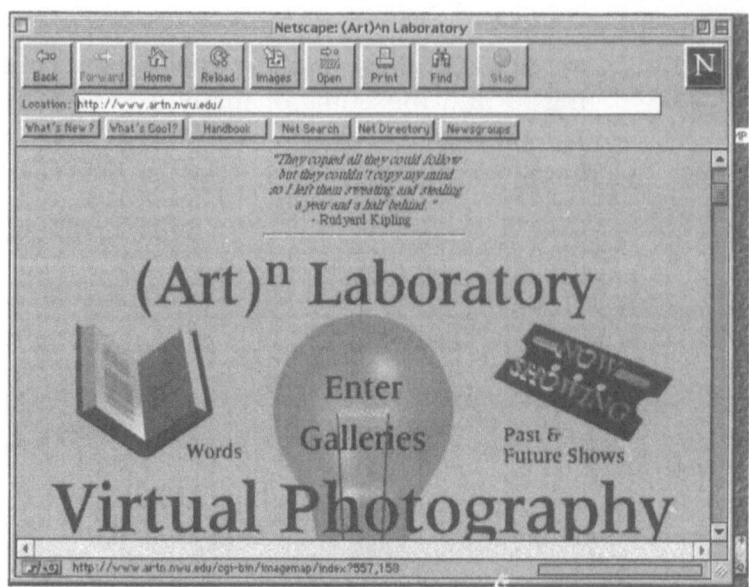

FIGURE 9.4.
The (art)^n
Laboratory Virtual
Photography exhibit.

times, and may not be to everyone's taste. On the other hand, the experience can be fun.

Check out The Asylum and the Creative Internet pages at the California Institute of Technology, `http://www.galcit.caltech.edu/~ta/cgi-bin/asylhome-ta` and `http:www.galcit.caltech.edu/~ta/creative.html`, respectively. These feature interesting items like interactive artworks, including a Lite Brite box you can play with over the Net, as well as an interactive TV index, a Websurfer guide, and an Internet polling booth.

CyberSight, at `http://cybersight.com/cgi-bin/cs/s?main.gmml`, is also worth taking a look at. It includes an interactive grafitti wall that you can embellish with your own graphics, hypermedia exhibits of different types, and links to interesting sites on the Web.

The Syracuse University Computer Graphics for the Arts home page (`http://ziris.syr.edu`) is another good site for collaborative Internet art exhibits of many types. It shows off the capabilities of Netscape for this type of interactive artwork to good effect. (See Figure 9.7.)

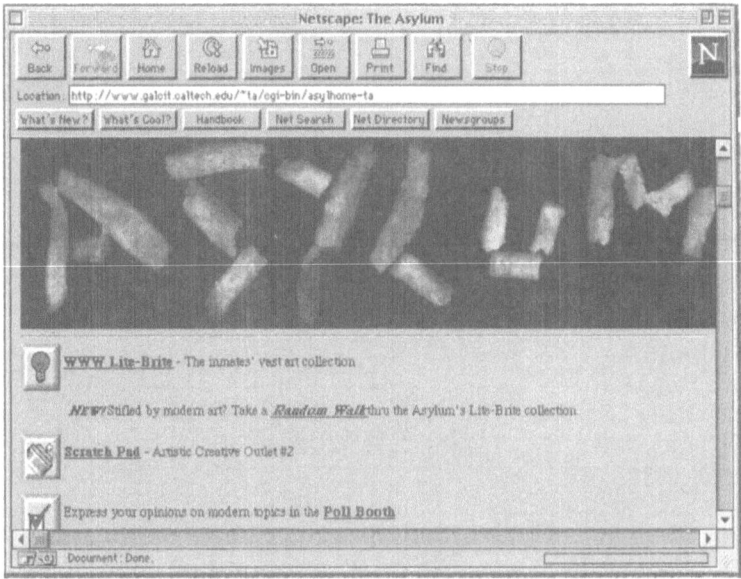

FIGURE 9.5.
The Asylum page at
CalTech.

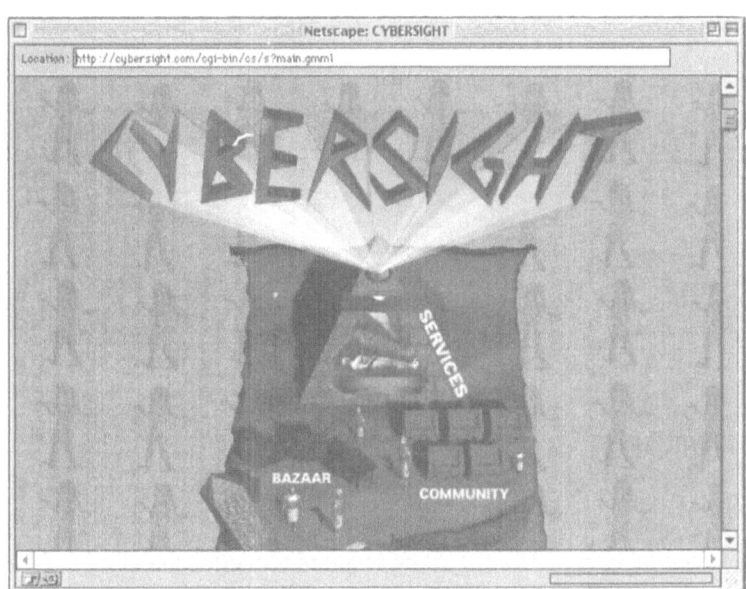

FIGURE 9.6.
The CyberSight
page.

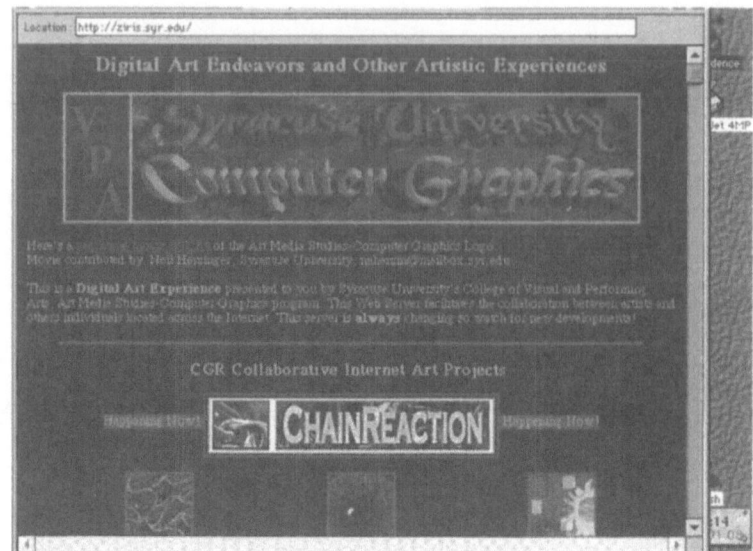

FIGURE 9.7.
The Syracuse
University Computer
Graphics for the Arts
home page.

The Geometry Center at the University of Minnesota features a Web site with interactive on-line geometry exhibits, including interactive models and game prototypes that you can explore with a Web browser like Netscape. It's at http://www.geom.umn.edu/apps/gallery.html.

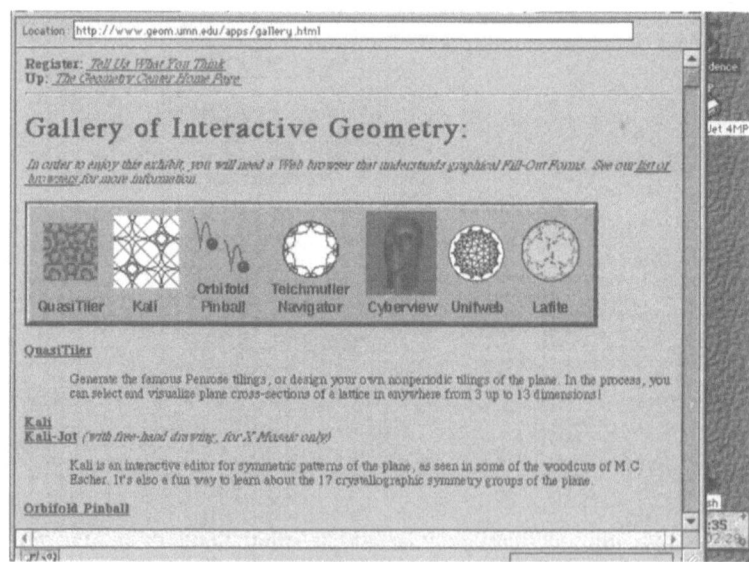

FIGURE 9.8.
The Geometry
Center at the
University of
Minnesota.

Comics on the Web

There's a lot of good information on comics on the Web. The best places to look for information are a couple of well-maintained comics-related home pages.

You can check out a comics archive at the University of Michigan that includes cover art from a variety of different comics types and eras. It provides a good look at how comics can be viewed across the Web. It's located at `http://www.css.itd.umich.edu/users/kens/comics.html`.

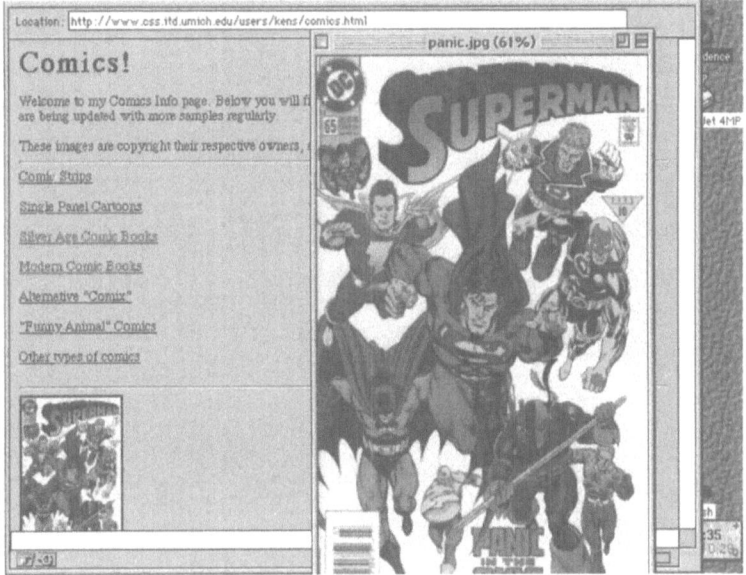

FIGURE 9.9.
The Comics archive at the University of Michigan.

Another site, the History of Comics page at `http://www.loa.com/~dsantos`, is dedicated to the history of the American comic book medium. It's also a good jumping-off point for comics-related information. (See Figure 9.10.)

Individual artists are also featured on the World Wide Web, ranging from Scott Adams' Dilbert comic strip (`http://nearnet.gnn.com/gnn/news/comix/dilbert.html`) to Tom Tomorrow's political satire This Modern World (`http://www.well.com/Community/comic`). Check out the NetCenter Comics on-line site (`http://www.netcenter.com/yellows/comics.html`) for more information and links. (See Figure 9.11.)

For an interesting look at how comics and the Web can inter-

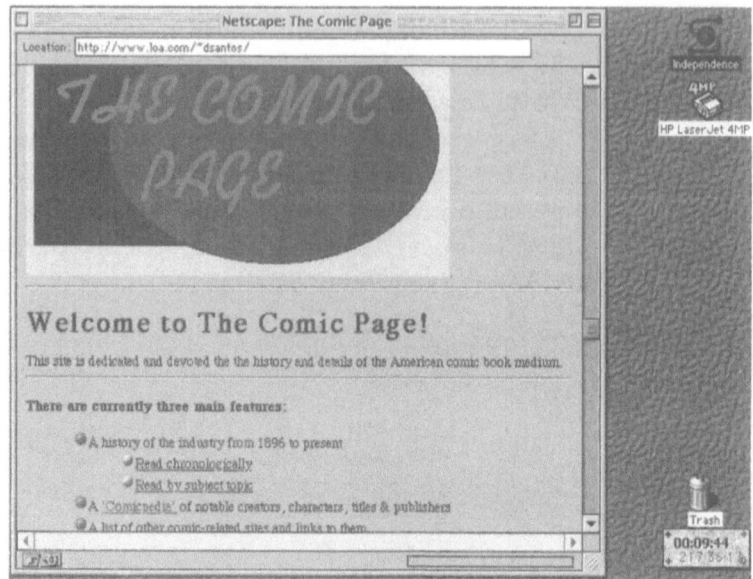

FIGURE 9.10.
The Comic Page
Web site.

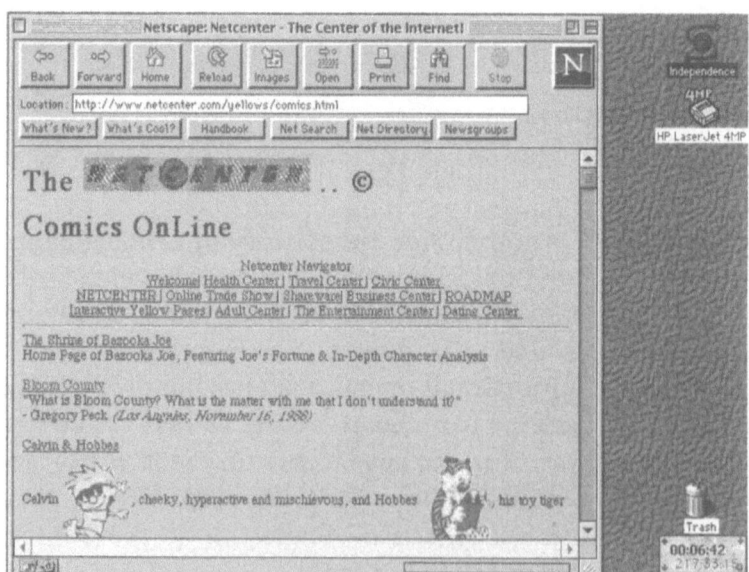

FIGURE 9.11.
The NetCenter
Comics on-line page.

act, the OncoLink Web server at the University of Pennsylvania has excerpts from the Harvey Pekar work "Our Cancer Year," a realistic portrait of the artist's struggle with cancer. The link for this is at `http://oncolink.upenn.edu/psycho_stuff/comics/index.html`.

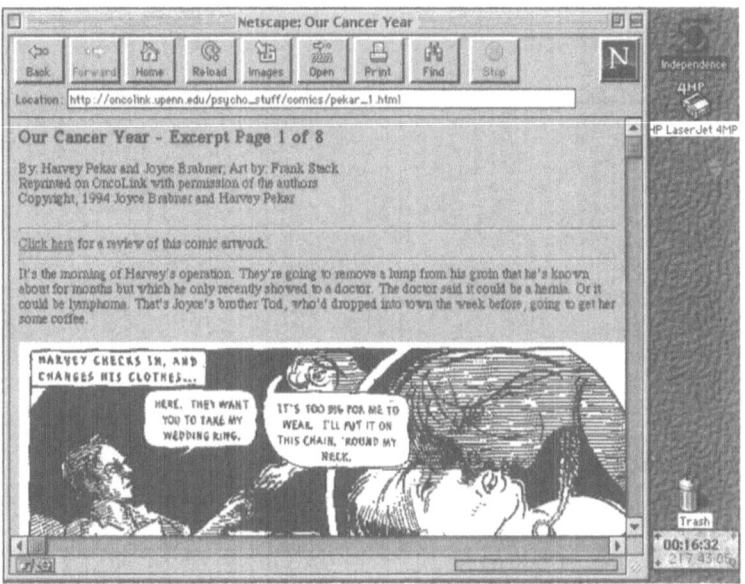

FIGURE 9.12.
Our Cancer Year
excerpt at OncoLink.

Games and Related Materials

Game information on the Internet ranges from home pages for different game systems to interactive games built right into the Web. As with the comics-related pages, the best places to start looking for information are on index pages maintained by individuals with a keen interest in gaming.

Michel Buffa's Video Games page at Carnegie-Mellon University (`http://www.cs.cmu.edu/afs/cs.cmu.edu/user/buffa/www/videogames.html`) is a good example. It includes links to information on game systems ranging from the SuperNintendo to the Atari Jaguar, the 3DO, and arcade machines. There's also a lot of links to the popular multiplatform game DOOM, and a hypertext version of the videogames FAQs (Frequently Asked Questions). (See Figure 9.13.)

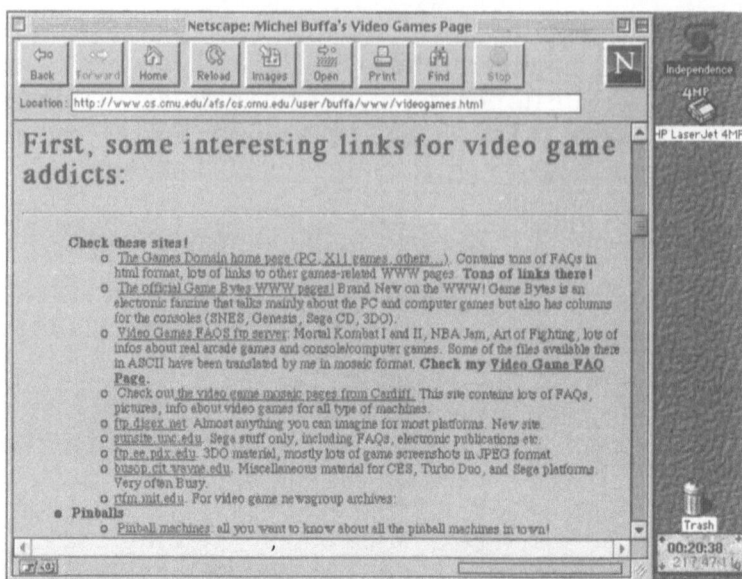

FIGURE 9.13.
Michel Buffa's Video
Games home page.

SEGA of America was one of the first game system companies to have their own home page on the Net. It features information on SEGA games and game platforms, JPEG images and MPEG movies from current and projected games, and game tips and tactics. Catch SEGA at `http://www.segaoa.com`. Of course, other game companies have made it to the Web, including Sony (`http://www.sony.com`), with a site devoted to the PlayStation.

For a look at a really cool game company, check out Rocket Science Games. Their site also features stills and MPEG movies from current and upcoming games. Rocket Science is at `http://www.rocketsci.com`.

Zarf's Interactive Games List is where you'll find links to most of the Net-specific games on the Internet. This site is very well laid out, and provides a good icon-based menu that lets you know the platform requirements for the different games. Games playable directly from Netscape and other Web browsers include Tarot and I Ching fortune-telling, Backgammon, Tic-Tac-Toe, Minesweeper, and more. There are also links to interactive quizzes and art projects. The Zarf list, also at Carnegie-Mellon University, is located at `http://www.cs.cmu/afs/andrew/org/kgb/zarf/www/games.html`.

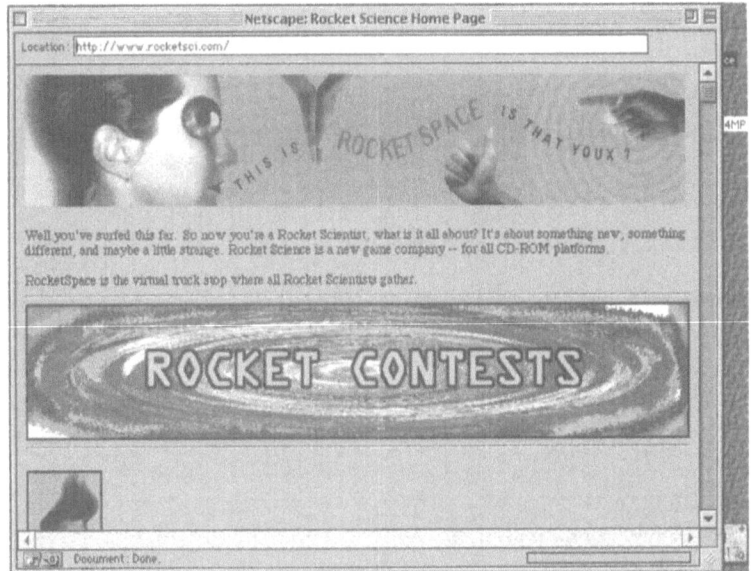

FIGURE 9.14.
Rocket Science
Games on the Web.

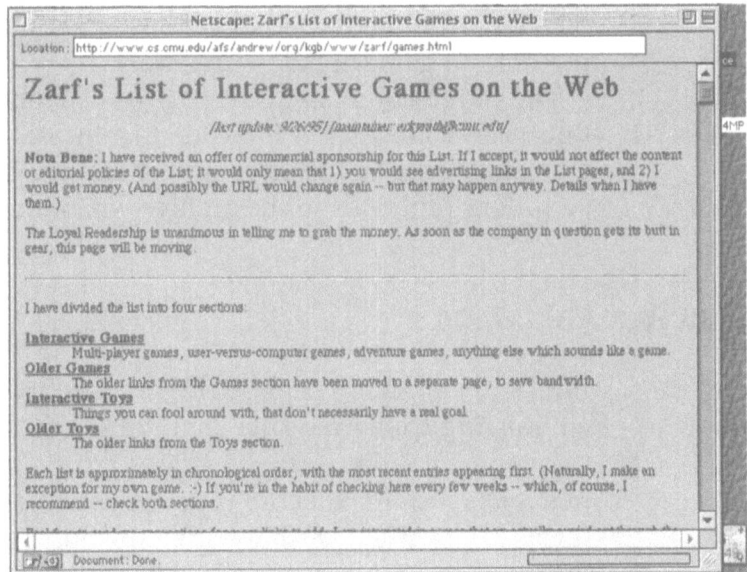

FIGURE 9.15.
The Zarf Interactive
Games home page.

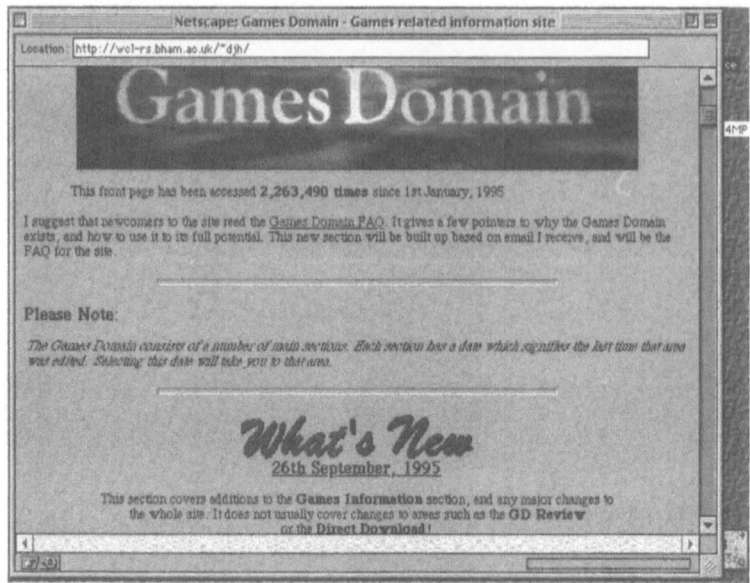

FIGURE 9.16.
The Games Domain
home page.

Games Domain (`http://wcl-rs.bham.ac.uk/~djh/`), located on a server in the United Kingdom, is another site with interesting links to games-related materials.

The Games Domain also has a list of Web sites where you can find shareware games for your Macintosh. Look in the Direct Download section for more information, including program descriptions and links to the archive where the files are located.

Film and Animation

Film and animation sites on the Internet are very well represented, ranging from Web sites maintained by major movie studios to computer animation collections from colleges and universities. Web sites for Viacom (`http://here.viacom.com`) and MCA (`http://www.mca.com`) have links to other sites for movie studios and television networks. These offer everything from online opening night participation to promotional material such as stills, MPEG video clips, and interactive multimedia software kits from current movie releases.

The deeper you get into films, the more you'll appreciate the excellent resources of the Internet Movie Database Browser. This site is a wealth of information on films, film directors, screen-

FIGURE 9.17.
Viacom's
Entertainment Index
of home pages.

writers, stars and their different roles, and production crews. It's set up almost exactly like a Veronica search engine, but with a custom Netscape interface that makes searching the movie database very intuitive. You can look up actors by name, and films by partial title, for example. It's easy to find a particular actor's roles or look up everything by a particular screenwriter in this database. The movie browser is very popular, so it's been replicated at several servers around the world for more immediate access. Users in the United States should use the site at the University of Mississippi. The home page for it is located at `http://www.msstate.edu/Movies/`.

Computer animation is featured in a number of interesting sites on the Web, including Cyberia, at the Hyperreal site (`http://www.hyperreal.com/cyberia`). Cyberia's Web site is directly related to their computer animation cable TV show, and it includes Web links to sites around the world featuring animation archives.

For comics-related animation, look at Rei's page at MIT (`http://www.mit.edu:8001/people/rei/home.html`). This site features comprehensive links to the world of Japanese animation (animae), including other home pages, file archives, episode guides, and fan magazines. (See Figure 9.18.)

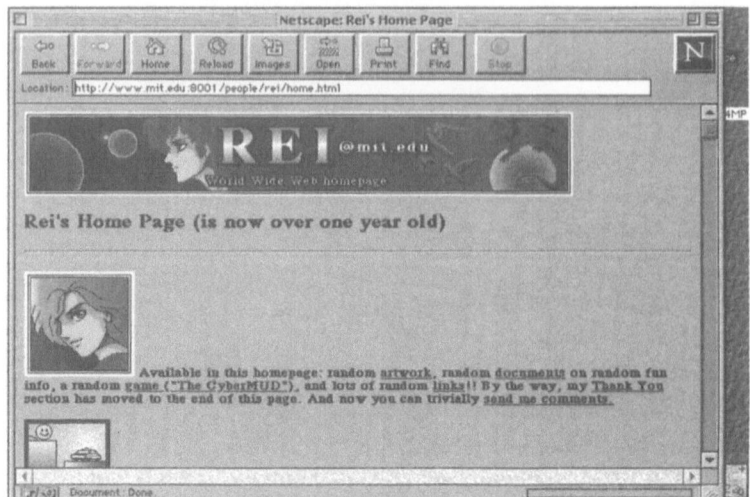

FIGURE 9.18.
Rei's home page at
MIT, focusing on
Japanese animation
(animae).

Music Sites

Some very comprehensive guides to music sites on the Internet
can be found at one or two sites, including the Internet Underground Music Archive (http://www.iuma.com) at Stanford University, and the Web Wide World of Music (http://american.
recordings.com/wwwofmusic/), maintained by American Record-
ings, Inc. Both feature links to bands all around the world, and
home pages that feature album cover art, digital music samples,
and concert information. The Web Wide World site also has a
link to the Ultimate Bands list, an alphabetical index to home
pages for various music artists all across the Internet. You can
also link your favorite band's site, if it's not already listed.

Other music sites you may want to try include EmeraldNet
(http://www.Emerald.NET), keepers of the Machines of Loving
Grace home page, the Virtual Radio archive (at http://www.
microserve.net/vradio), and Motown Records (at http://www
.musicbase.co.uk/music/motown).

This is just a sample of the music resources available over the
Internet; you'll also want to look at the Virtual Library's Music
section, located on a server in Finland at http://www.oulu.fi/
music.html, and also the music subcategory of the Entertainment section at Yahoo.

FIGURE 9.19.
The Internet
Underground Music
Archive Web site.

FIGURE 9.20.
The Netscape
FishCam.

Miscellaneous Unclassifiable Fun and Toys

Practically unclassifiable are some of the more interesting Internet sites. The Lego page is one of these; it includes information on building kits, instruction sheets, and contest information. It also includes specialty items like reports on tours of the Lego factory and on MIT's Lego robots courses. Find it at `http://legowww.homepages.com`.

A pair of interesting interactive sites are the Trojan Room Coffee Machine at Cambridge University (`http://www.cl.cam.ac.uk/coffee/coffee.html`) and the Amazing FishCam at Netscape Communications (`http://www.netscape.com/fishcam/`). These take photographs of their respective subjects at round-the-clock intervals and put the photos up on their servers. At any time, you can check on the status of a coffeepot in England or on a fish tank in Northern California. Remember, if you can't see anything, the lights may be turned out.

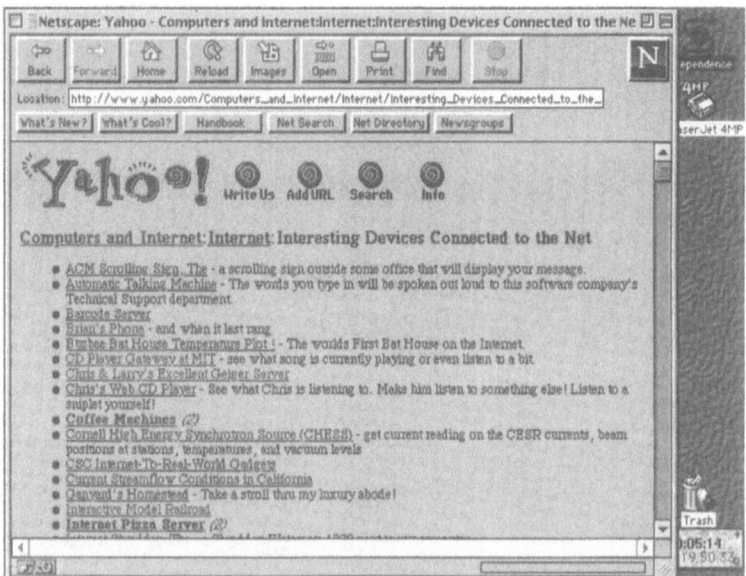

FIGURE 9.21.
The Interesting Devices page at Yahoo.

Find more interactive World Wide Web machines at Yahoo, in the Computers and Internet: Internet section called Interesting Devices Connected to the Net. These include spy cameras, model railroads, interactive robots, appliances, TV views and even people's up- to-date Mac desktop screen captures that you can view and interact with.

10
Serious Productivity

If you're looking for Internet resources on a more serious note, you can find a wealth of information on business, including investment risk analysis and stock information, as well as a vast collection of weather-related information, and also several interesting Web servers being run by government agencies.

Business Centers and Information Services

The Internet has several good centers for business. A central site is at the University of Texas server maintained by Professor James Garven. The RISKWeb at U. Texas (`http://www.riskweb.html`) is aimed at providing World Wide Web insurance risk information, and includes links to several important sites, including on-line documentation and statistics. Its FINWeb counterpart (`http://www.finweb.html`) is a Financial Economics server with more general links to finance issues. (See Fig. 10.1.)

There are also indices to business sites on the Web. These include collections like CommerceNet (focusing on commercial Internet sites), at `http://www.commerce.net`, and IndustryNet (focusing on the manufacturing industry), at `http://www.industry.net`, as well as a large Business and Economy index at Yahoo, `http://www.yahoo.com/Business_and_Economy/`. (See Fig. 10.2.)

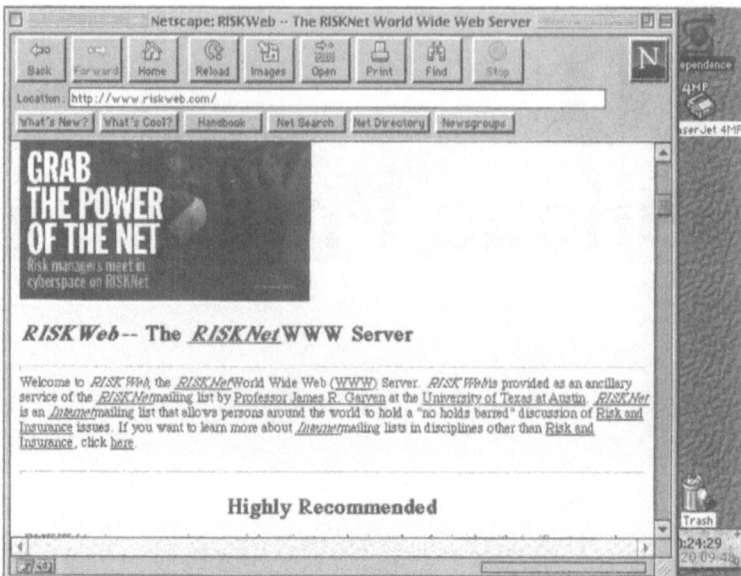

FIGURE 10.1.
RISKWeb.

FIGURE 10.2.
IndustryNet home
page.

Also on the University of Texas server, the Kiwi Club (`http://kiwiclub.bus.utexas.edu/finance/kiwiserver/kiwiserver.html`) maintains a comprehensive Web site with many good links to financial lecture information, bank and corporate sites, and commercial companies on the World Wide Web.

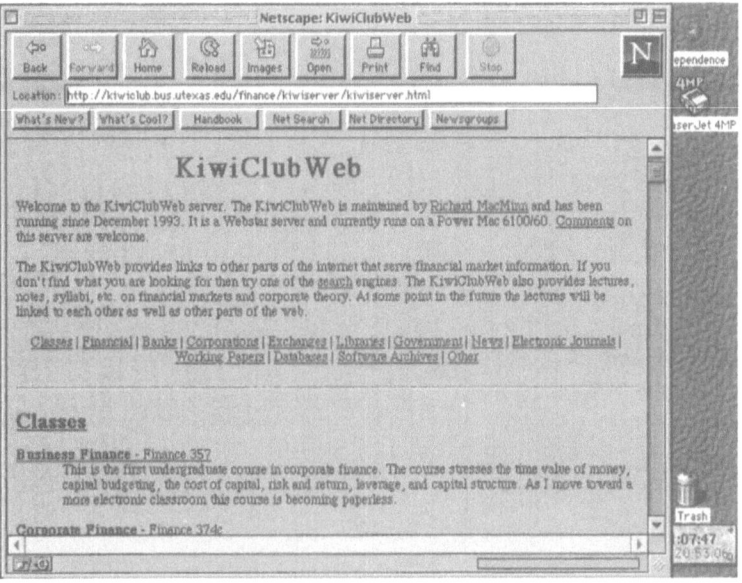

FIGURE 10.3.
The Kiwi Club Web site at the University of Texas.

The Business Webliography also features a World Wide Web guide to business sites, issues, and information on the Internet. You'll find it at a server at Louisiana State University, at `http://www.lib.lsu.edu/bus/index.html`. It provides a good overview of business resources on the Net in a hypertext subject guide. (See Fig. 10.4.)

GNN's Whole Internet Catalog business listings (`http://gnn.com/gnn/wic/bus.toc.html`) include subtopic links to Web sites on agriculture, career and employment services, entrepreneurship and small business information, Internet commerce, investment and management houses, nonprofit organizations, personal finance, and real estate matters.

Also at GNN, the Personal Finance Center (`http://gnn.com:80/meta/finance/`) provides a collection of resources for the private investor, including articles on how to invest wisely and links to stock quote retrieval systems and mutual fund information. (See Fig. 10.5.)

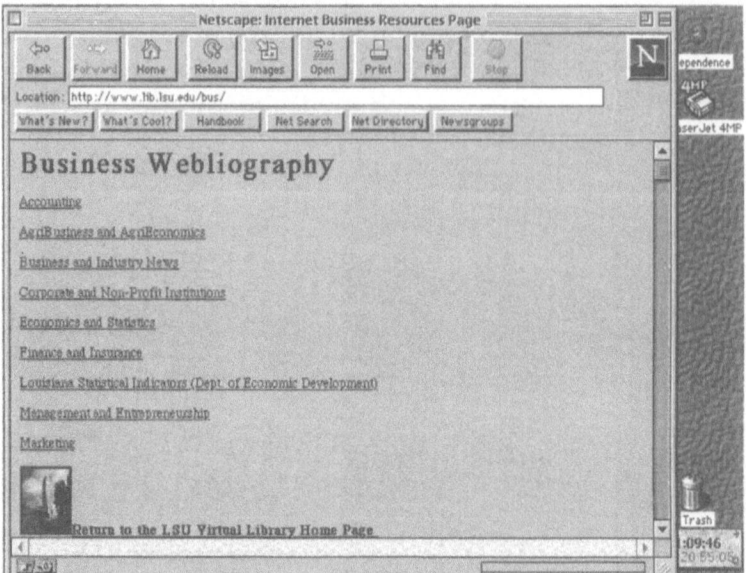

FIGURE 10.4.
The Business
Webliography at
Louisiana State
University.

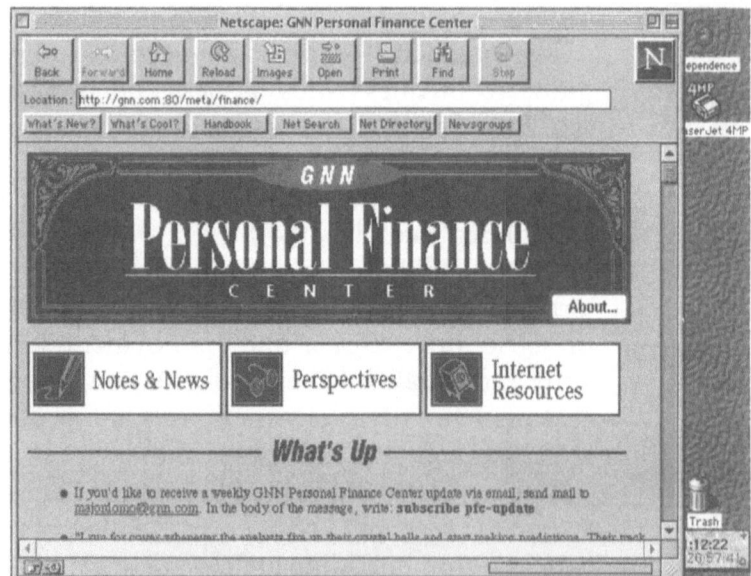

FIGURE 10.5.
The GNN Personal
Finance Center.

Netscape Communications' What's Cool page has a link to the Rensselaer Polytechnic University short list of interesting business sites on the World Wide Web (`http://www.rpi.edu/~okeefe/business.html`); this features a prescreened list of no more than 50 businesses deemed worthy of inclusion to the list because of superior presentation, suitability of the Web as a medium for their business, and other criteria. It's a good place to find interesting Web sites directly.

You can also try the Open Market on-line Guide to Commercial Services on the Net (`http://www.directory.net`), as well as the Internet Business Center (`http://www.tig.com/IBC/index.html`), and GNN's Commercial Business listings (`http://gnn.com/gnn/bus/index.html`), for more information on commercial corporations on the Net.

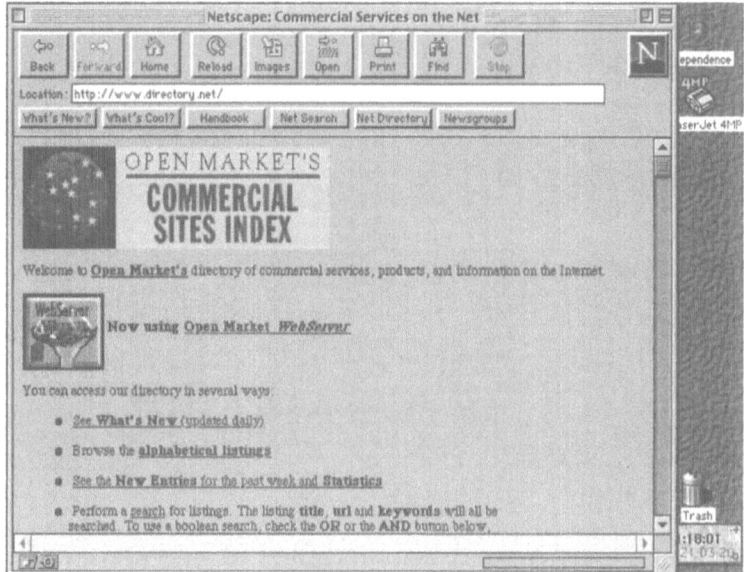

FIGURE 10.6.
The Open Market Guide to Commercial Sites on the Internet.

Banks and Investment Houses

There are many banks and investment houses on the Internet, and you can use an index like the Kiwi Club at the University of Texas listed above to access them. Two representative examples include the Wells Fargo Bank Web site (`http://www.wellsfargo.com`), which features an alphabetical index to the bank's services and multimedia sound and picture files of the bank's history, and the J.P. Morgan investment house (`http://www.jpmorgan.com/`), which also features an index to Morgan's services on the Web, as well as a link to an interactive Web application called RiskMetrics (used for market risk management).

FIGURE 10.7.
The Wells Fargo
Bank Web site.

You may also find the Chicago Mercantile Exchange Web site useful, at `http://www.cme.com`.

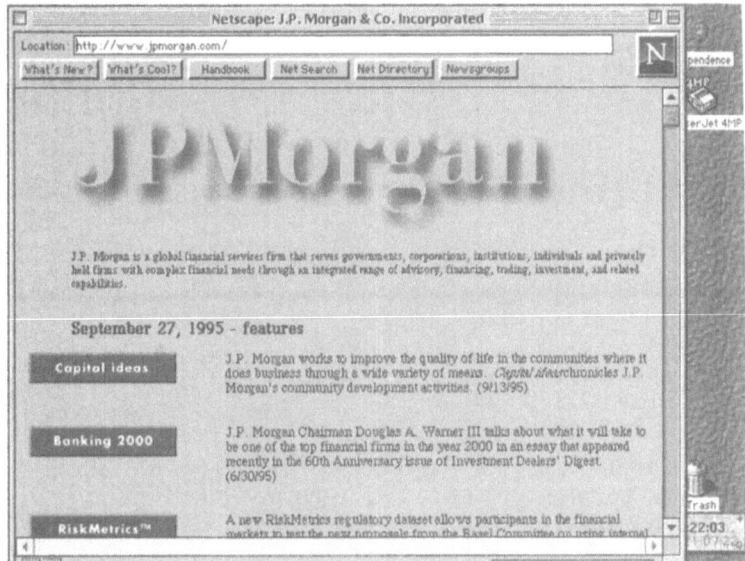

FIGURE 10.8.
The J.P. Morgan investment house home page.

Government Web Sites

The University of Texas RISKWeb site also includes a page with a Government World Wide Web server list that includes links to the FedWorld Federal information system, as well as home pages for the White House, the FBI, the Department of Commerce, and the Social Security Administration. You can find further government information at the U.S. Patent and Trademark Office site (http://www.uspto.gov) and the Small Business Administration Online service (http://www.sbaonline.sba.gov), and a large collection of Federal links at FedWorld, http://www.fedworld.com.

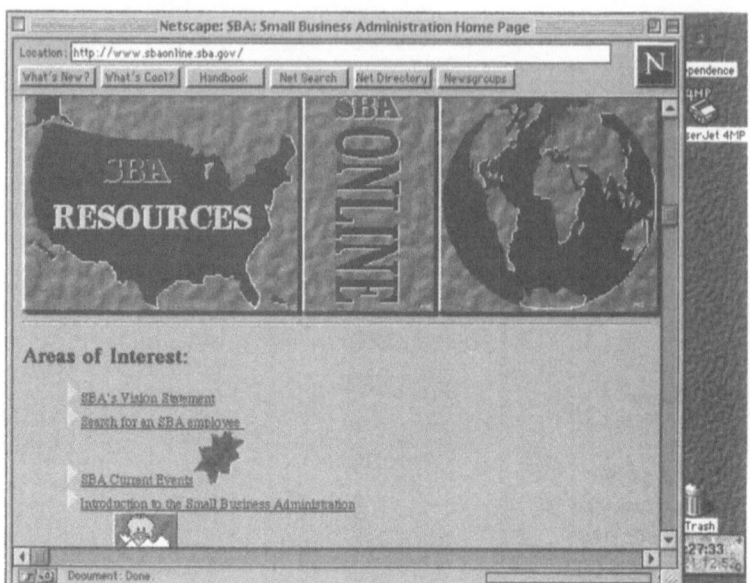

FIGURE 10.9.
The Small Business
Administration
Online.

Utilities and Services

Business services include the DowVision information retrieval system of articles from The Wall Street Journal (go to `http://dowvision.wais.net` for a trial version), and Security APL's stock quote interface, which lets you look up time-delayed market quotes by entering in the appropriate market symbols. The PAWWS (Portfolio Accounting World Wide—Security APL) home page is located at `http://pawws.secapl.com`, and it also features information like SEC filings. You can get to the quote server directly at `http://www.secapl.com/cgi-bin/qs`.

The NetWorth Personal Investment service page, a subscription service with information on over 5000 mutual funds, is located at `http://networth.galt.com`.

The Maxwell Labs Taxing Times server provides on-line tax information, including electronic forms available for downloading. It's located at `http://www.scubed.com/tax/tax.html`.

You can check on Federal Express packages by entering a FedEx airbill number in the form at the `http://www.fedex.com` server site. A report on the shipment's progress will be displayed. It's a good application that shows how useful the World Wide Web

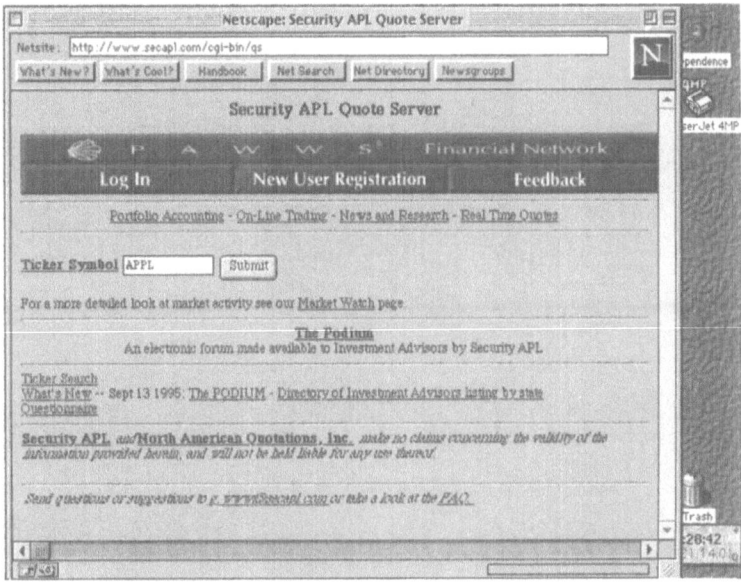

FIGURE 10.10.
The Security APL
stock quotes server.

can be for day-to-day activities. Also try the United Parcel Service (`http://www.ups.com`) and the U.S. Post Office (`http://www.usps.gov`) for more on-line tracking systems and shipping information.

The University of Buffalo CEDAR Project address server, at `http://www.cedar.buffalo.edu/adserv.html`, features a forms-based application that looks up ZIP codes based on address information you enter into a text panel. It can also generate a downloadable PostScript label of your result (complete with a bar code) that you can print directly to an envelope, which will expedite your mail.

Maps, Weather, and Geography

Weather information on the World Wide Web is divided between University sites and government installations. The Weather Server (`http://thunder.atms.purdue.edu`) at Purdue University is a great place to find up-to-date satellite photos and detailed weather maps.

You can also try `http://www.atmos.uiuc.edu` for The Daily Planet from the University of Illinois at Champaign-Urbana's Atmospheric Sciences department, another good site for weather-related information.

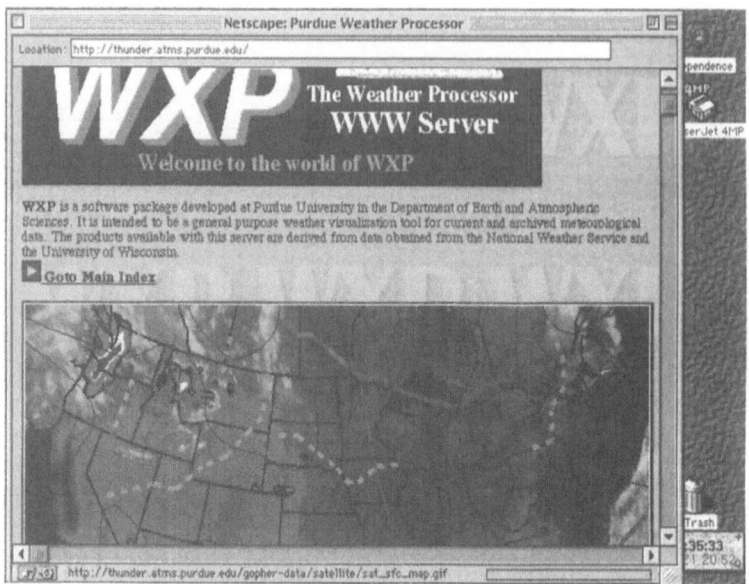

FIGURE 10.11.
The Purdue Weather
Server.

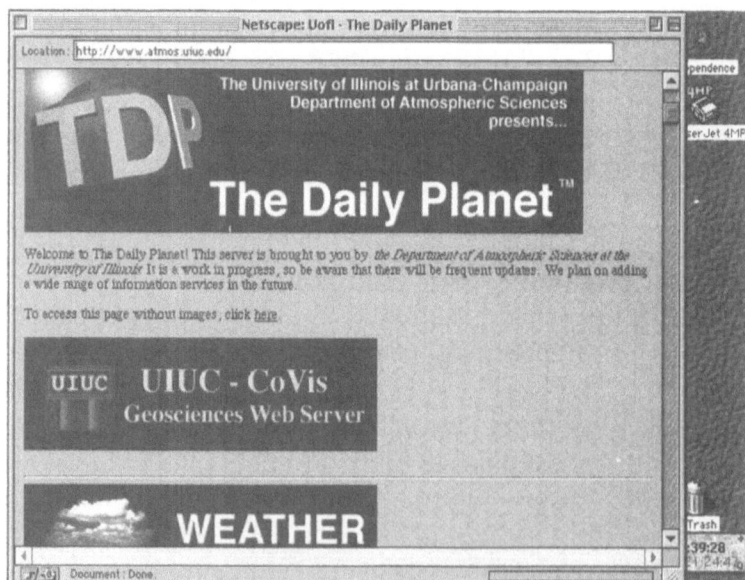

FIGURE 10.12.
The Daily Planet at
the University of
Illinois.

Government sites usually specialize in more in-depth meteorological data. A coordinating project is the National Science Foundations' UNIDATA service (`http://atm.geo.nsf.gov`), a way to tie comprehensive weather data together in real time between sites. You can also access comprehensive weather satellite photo archives at the National Climactic Data Center (`http://www.ncdc.noaa.gov/ncdc.html`), as well as weather-related government databases.

The East and West Coast sites of the United States Geological Survey provide good environmental information They're at `http://bramble.er.usgs.gov` (Woods Hole USGS, Atlantic Marine Survey) and `http://walrus.wr.usgs.gov` (Pacific Marine Geology Survey). respectively.

The interactive map at the Xerox Parc (Palo Alto Research Center) is an interesting example of how the World Wide Web can display cartographic information. The map displayed can zoom in on a region by clicking on a specific area, and you can also search for a region by keywords. The Xerox map is located at `http://pubweb.parc.xerox.com/map`.

Another interesting usage of maps is located at the Southern California Department of Transportation site at `http://www.scubed.com/caltrans/transnet.html`. This site shows detailed maps of traffic patterns along major roadways in Southern California and updates its maps from roadbed sensors as the day progresses, showing particular average speeds along certain stretches of road. This makes it very easy to visualize traffic jams and plan for areas to avoid. This site also provides links to map servers for other locations around the world.

FIGURE 10.13.
Pacific Marine
Geology Survey.

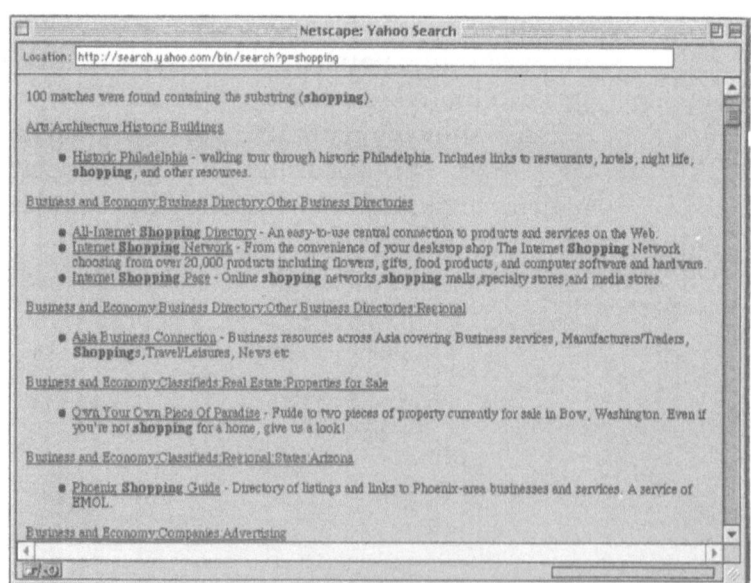

FIGURE 10.14.
Yahoo on-line
shopping links.

Shopping

Shopping on the Internet is starting to swing into full gear. Try searching the index at Yahoo for the term "shopping" for plenty of on-line commercial sites and Internet malls.

With online credit card transaction security a real concern, you'll have to be careful about using some of the these shopping networks directly. They do offer on-line catalog interfaces that work well, however, and many of the services do business over the telephone. A representative example is the Internet Shopping Network, at `http://www.internet.net`.

FIGURE 10.15.
The Internet
Shopping Network.

You'll also find shopping services located at major on-line sites like GNN (`http://gnn.com`) listed through Internet business directories like those listed previously.

11
Closing Considerations

Netscape continues to develop versions of their browser for the Mac platform. Future plans are to include support of native Apple technologies like QuickTime and QuickTimeVR directly inside Netscape, so you'll be able to watch movies and move through QTVR scenes without having to launch an external viewer.

Netscape 2.0's support for plug-in programs means that developers will be able also to add functionality directly to the program. Netscape plans to work closely with companies like Macromedia to include support for Designer presentations, and Adobe to support the Acrobat standard. Strategic partnerships with companies that have had a long appreciation for the Mac platform bodes well for the future development of advanced versions of Netscape for Macintosh.

Java is a new technology developed by Sun Microsystems that allows small "applets" to be embedded directly inside a Web browser page. These can include real-time calculation programs (mini-spreadsheets), fast interactive animations, and games. Netscape has pledged to include support for Java in the final (non-beta) release of Navigator 2.0 on all platforms, including Macintosh. Find out more about it at http://java.sun.com, including Sun's own plans for a port of the prototype HotJava browser to Macintosh.

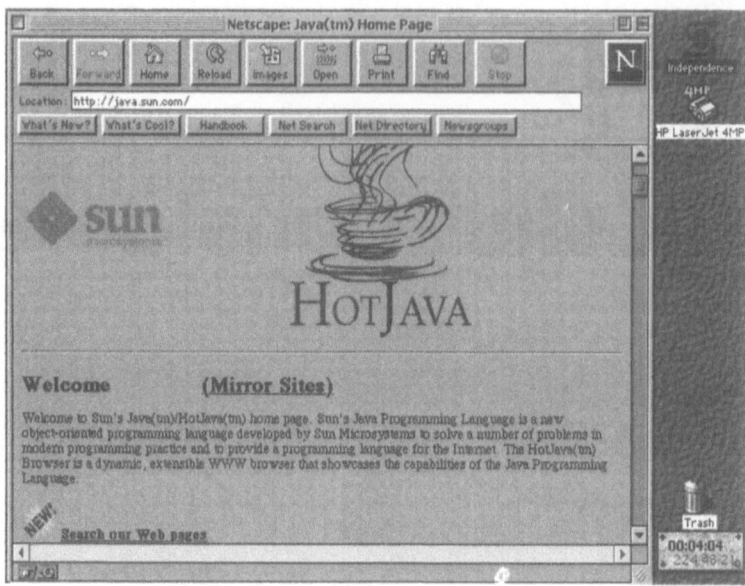

FIGURE 11.1.
The Java home page.

Apple's future plans include the development of a browser prototype that includes support for the OpenDoc standard. OpenDoc allows software to be made of specialized parts that can communicate independently; their Cyberdog demo showed a Web browser that included an embedded spreadsheet that could update itself across the Net. Apple has a lot of documentation on the OpenDoc standard on its tech info and developer support Web site, at `http://www.info.apple.com`.

The Open Transport networking protocol will be fully integrated with PPP, and Apple plans to continue to work to maintain compatibility with future new hardware technology (including standard PCI bus support). Apple has documentation on Open Transport at its main Web sites.

Expect Apple's new Copland operating system to provide a powerful platform for Netscape. Improved 32-bit performance will allow smoother graphics handling and better support for multiple interacting programs. You'll also be able to set up Copland to change the overall look of your MacOS; this will in turn change the basic way Netscape will look, to match your new desktop. We've used a shareware program called Aaron to give a base Copland-like look to our System 7.5 desktop for this book (find it at the main Mac shareware sites), but you'll also be able to make some significant changes, like in the prototype

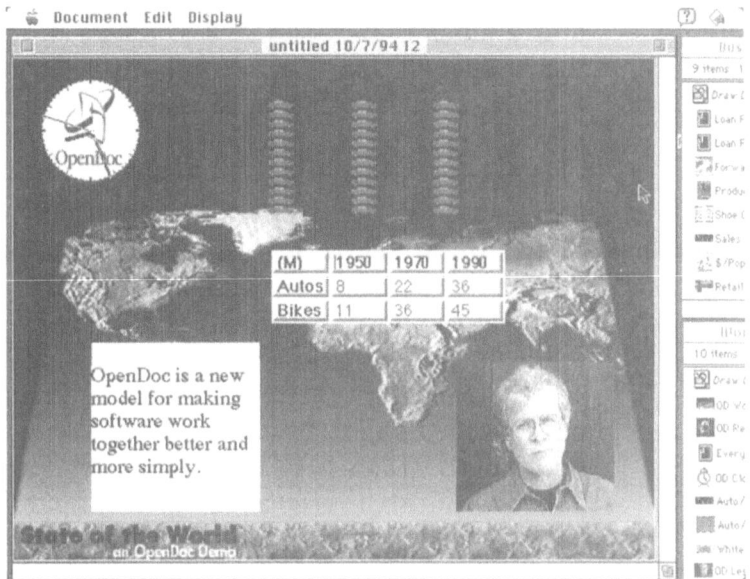

FIGURE 11.2.
A look at OpenDoc.

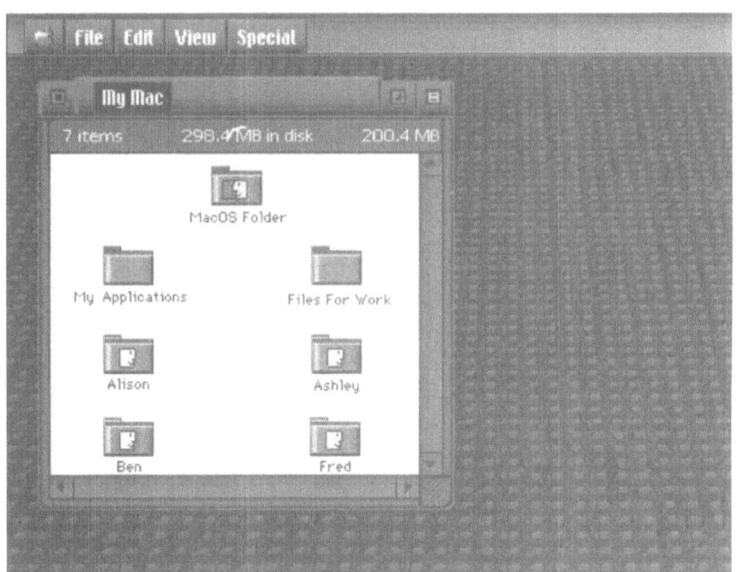

FIGURE 11.3.
A specialized look
for the Copland
interface.

shown in Figure 11.3. (Apple is using the codenames Copland and Gershwin for future versions of the MacOS; they must be music fans. The creator of the Aaron program is following in their footsteps—can George and Ira be far behind?)

Third-party developers are also working hard to include new technologies for Mac Web browsers. One of the more interesting efforts is in the area of VRML, the Virtual Reality Markup Language. This will allow users to interact with virtual scenes directly in a Web browser over the Net. Demos have included on-line museums and architectural walk-throughs you can navigate in 3D. Future plans will include interactive meeting places that will allow users to interact in 3D space with other users, in realms created by Web providers. The main VRML developers have pledged support for the Mac platform; see the VRML Web site at `http://www.vrml.org` for more information (or search at Yahoo for VRML). A representative company that has announced a Mac VRML browser is WorldView, at `http://www.webmaster.com/vrml/`. You should be able to download prototype VRML Mac browsers from these sites as well.

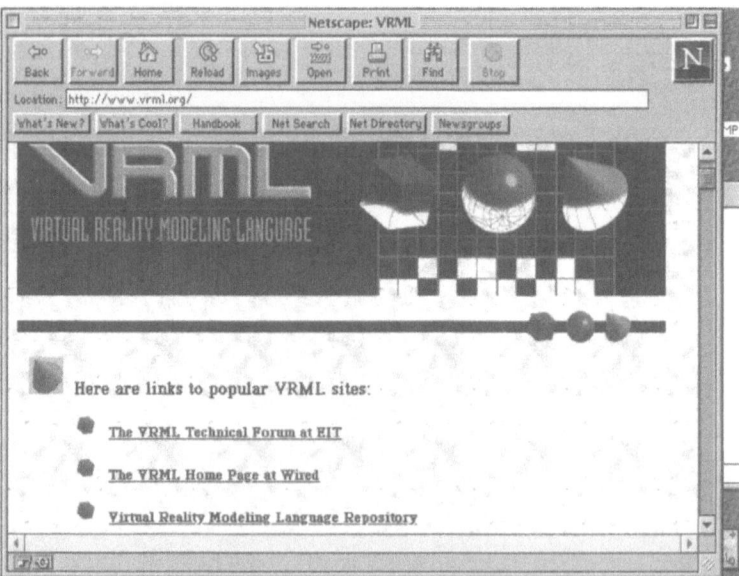

FIGURE 11.4.
VRML on the Web.

The Mac platform will continue to grow and flourish as the best OS for users that want to get the most out of their systems without encountering unnecessary hardship. This will work well with the development of more powerful versions of Netscape, including Apple technologies and open standards, by keeping the software and hardware free from complexity. Navigating the Net is certainly easier when your system is preconfigured to handle multimedia, and Internet access is available with several instant start-up packages and a number of providers to choose from. Macintosh will continue to be the best system for the net-savvy future.

Index